TANKER

Boys, Men, and Cowards

Edward C. Luzinas

ATHENA PRESS
LONDON

TANKER
Boys, Men, and Cowards
Copyright © Edward C. Luzinas 2004

ISBN 1 932077 53 7

First Published 2004 by
ATHENA PRESS
Queen's House, 2 Holly Road
Twickenham TW1 4EG
United Kingdom

Printed for Athena Press

TANKER
Boys, Men, and Cowards

Dedicated to the boys who became m en as front-line troops. They shed their blood, sweat, and tears assaulting and conquering each and every yard of enemy-held soil in the hell they call WAR.

Acknowledgement and Special Thanks

To the cannon fodder of September–October 1944—participants of the Palau Campaign. Their recollections made this book possible.

THANKS

Foreword

December 7, 1941: the youth of our neighborhood, a poor working community, had gathered in our favorite center, a pool room, to pass away the time for the lack of money and better things to do. While shooting pool and listening to the professional football game on the radio, our entertainment was interrupted by the announcement that the Japanese nation had bombed Hawaii in a sneak attack on Pearl Harbor. The Japs had bombed Pearl Harbor.

We quit shooting pool. The question? What is Pearl Harbor? Where is Pearl Harbor? Are we at war with Japan? With these developments, what did the future have in store for us? What was our fate and destiny to be?

We were soon to find out.

On December 8, 1941, the day after the Pearl Harbor attack, the President of the United States of America, Franklin Delano Roosevelt, asked Congress to declare war on the Japanese nation. We were now at war with Japan. On December 11, 1941, Japan's Axis partners, Italy and Germany, declared war on the United States; Congress reciprocated. We were now totally and fully involved in World War II on a global scale.

Preface

My book, my memoirs, hopefully relates the lives and experiences of the fine boys who proved themselves men. Men who helped make unbearable experiences bearable in the conquest of Angaur and Peleliu, islands of the Palau Group on the road to Japan.

Tanker is a factual account of the General Sherman tank named "Champagne", numbered C5 of the 710th Tank Battalion, Army of The United States. Its complement:

Commander, Lieutenant Harol

Driver, Technical Sergeant 4th (T4) Bill Williams

Assistant Driver, T4 Harold "Ike" Grieb

Gunner, Corporal Ed "Fats" Luzinas

Radio man and assistant gunner, Private 1st Class Forest "Lightning" Kern.

Contents

1: Civilians—Recruits and Basic Training

In September 1940, Congress approved the Selective Training and Service Act. It was the first peacetime draft in American history.

We now had a new crop of cannon fodder for the "grim reaper": the graduating class of 1941. After graduation I earned good money doing defense work, building steam locomotives, then working on the General Sherman Tank.

Our country went into total mobilization. I was called up for the mental and physical examination at the Induction Center. During this processing, the Recruiting Sergeant asked us to please be orderly and take our oath. We were obedient, raised our right hands and were sworn in. We were then asked to take one step forward. Being boys we started discussing the events of this movement. The Sergeant then barked at us to keep our "…fuckin' traps shut! You're in the Army now!" We were then given ten days to tidy up our affairs.

After terminating employment, the partying and the goodbyes, we, the "New Recruits", gathered at the railroad station and departed for our destination, Camp Upton on Long Island, New York, an Army Reception Center. There we were outfitted and given our Intelligence Quotient and final determination as to where and best (what outfit or unit) we could serve our country.

I was eighteen years of age, fat—extremely fat, with a 46-inch girth or waistline—and the Army did not have the woolen olive drab (ODs) for me, so they could not ship me out to my assigned unit. This Reception Center procedure of arrival, testing, out-fitting and shipping normally took three days at that time. It took the Army at Camp Upton forty-five days to get me pants so I could be completely outfitted; then they could ship me out to my assigned unit: North Camp Polk, Louisiana, an Armored Division Training Camp. Camp Polk is located in the north-western region of the state of Louisiana close to the border of Texas. It's a vast, desolate area, an ideal place in which to train soldiers. The "soldiers" of our newly formed 8th

Armored Division were boys, the average age being nineteen. The Army, with its systems and methods, was now going to indoctrinate these boys and hope to have men as their finished product. This procedure started at six o'clock in the middle of the night. Our "sweet" First Sergeant with his plaything, my nemesis to this present day (I still jump when I hear one), the police whistle, would come into our barracks and give out a ghastly shriek with his whistle. I know he enjoyed this moment, it made his day: Reveille, fall out for roll-call.

You lined up in front of your barracks, the Company Assembly Area. The Company Commander, a Captain from a Southern State, came out, faced the boys and told the First Sergeant to report. It sounded to me like "go back to bed". I was ready and willing to obey this command, but no such luck: the First Sergeant then reported that we were all present or accounted for and saluted the Captain.

We then fell out of this assembly and got ready for chow (breakfast) at the mess hall—an area designated for the preparation, serving and consumption of your sustenance (ration of food to sustain life). After this "culinary treat" you were told to clean your barracks, then fall out and police (clean) the Company Area. You had to pick up anything movable, and if that was not possible, to paint it. The litter was normally cigarette butts that were not field stripped.

That was the start of my two-year, 350-day stint with the Army of the United States. The Army would now use their processes to make us into killers—hired killers. I cursed and swore at the methods then, and still do. But I believe it is an absolute necessity if you are to have effective combat troops.

The activation and forming of the 8th Armored Division began with the arrival of our cadre, skilled troops especially selected to train others. My unit, 1st Platoon, I Company, 80th Armored Regiment, had as Cadre Staff Sergeant John Saddler, a man about 5' 5" tall; Buck Sergeant Ronald Hartley, 6' 3" tall, the Hollywood version of a combat soldier; and Willard, Buck Sergeant, a quiet, hard-working, reserved man.

Our Company Commander, a Captain who was a crackerjack training officer, knew his tanks and loved to drive them. Our other officers were second looeys fresh out of OCS. As we were taught, so were they. Many second looeys were trained in our company, then transferred to other companies, or if found to be unsatisfactory sent to repple depple (replacement center) for reassignment. These officers had no direct bearing on our unit. Our permanent assigned Company Officers were to enter the picture later, in the training of the recruits. The immediate and outstanding of these recruits were Forest "Lightning" Kern and Karle, both to later prove to be a blessing for our platoon. And of course the other extreme was present—notably a guy named Alvin, a real asshole who used to count cadence and march in the barracks, trying to score brownie points. Another guy, a bigoted ass named Raub, tried to push his weight around.

In the Army you always work in pairs. Two men, who could each depend on the other. This was called the "Buddy System". It was very beneficial in combat, or other situations—a prime requirement. "Lightning" and I teamed up as buddies.

The organization of the First Platoon, my Platoon, to which I shall devote the major portion of my recollections, began. The first promotions occurred. I was named Acting Corporal of the First Squad. Karle was in charge of the Second Squad, and Alvin the Third Squad. Alvin's brown-nosing was paying off.

I was the 1st Squad Leader of the First Platoon, placing emphasis on the leader bit, which shall be explained. My duties were to report all present or accounted for of my Squad at roll-call and to assist and report to Sergeant Saddler. The one and only incident of "command" occurred during barracks cleaning one Friday night prior to Saturday Inspection. Our Company Commander, on a sneak inspection, found me scrubbing floors on my hands and knees. The Captain called me aside and notified me that I was a Squad Leader and as such to direct my men and that I was not required to perform menial tasks. I told the Captain that I was the Squad Leader, not the Squad Pusher; I would work and my squad would follow. After that, I was in like Flynn; I could do no wrong. My Company was no longer composed of rich boys or poor boys; we were now GIs (Government Issue), all wearing the same clothing and consuming the same chow, as we began our basic training. The Army was hoping to make men out of boys, and while so doing create an effective combat unit.

The crux of Basic Training was: the Army will now show you—how to—when to—and where to—have a bowel movement by the numbers. They, the Army, shall also tell you where to place these feculent excrements.

It began: you shall go through what will be your defined procedures during all phases of your military training. These are: Reveille, roll-call, chow, police-up, calisthenics, close order drill (precision marching), and schooling (brainwashing). The system works. After sixteen weeks of this the skinny kids put on weight and develop muscles, us fat boys sweat the fat out of us and get down to Army weight. They teach and order you to snap shit (come to attention, and to salute the uniform of an officer). The officers are usually eggheads (requirement of IQ 110 or higher) with highly inflated egos. Vainglorious creatures, normally fresh out of Officers' Candidate School (OCS), these officers taught us the rudiments and protocol of military life, while they themselves also learned. Remember, our country was now undergoing full mobilization. Our Company was the training ground for these officers, one quiet and reserved, one friendly, one over-friendly—the usual flamboyant one who became known as "the Phony", and "the Penis". These officers brainwashed us naive kids.

We sweated in the heat of a Louisiana summer, did our KP, dug slit trenches (latrines—storage of feculent excrements) walked our posts on guard duty and learned how to apply a condom to a simulated penis—a broom handle—and how to take preventative measures against venereal diseases. We were learning soldiering.

Next in our military careers came our introduction to the weapons made by man to kill man: our tanks.

2: Advanced Training

The Army doctrine is when you receive an order, comply. If there is any question, do it first, then question it.

First Platoon Sergeant Sadler faced his platoon and stated that when we receive an order from him or his Buck Sergeant do it— don't give him any crap or he would climb our frames. They (our Cadre) would now introduce us to and acquaint us with our primary weapon, the tank.

The General Sherman Tank, M4, was a thirty-two-ton monster made of armored steel, molded, no rivets. The thickness of this armor was three inches on the front and turret—the vital spots; and two and a half inches thick on the sides of the tank. The belly and the engine compartment were the vulnerable, highly vulnerable, weaknesses. It was propelled on tracks by a twelve-cylinder radial air-cooled engine, a Whirlwind Cyclone airplane gasoline engine. Going downhill the tank could attain a speed of twenty-three m.p.h. with an eighty-mile range. During the North African Campaign, the First Armored Division took heavy casualties using riveted tanks. The rivets pop out when a tank is hit by artillery fire. Any projectile that penetrates the tank's armor ricochets around and remains inside the tank as it has used up its penetrating force and cannot exit the tank or enclosure. The tank operates on its gasoline-driven engines and it stores about 100 gallons. It stores 100 rounds of 75 millimeter (three inches in diameter) artillery ammunition, thousands of 30 and 50 caliber machine-gun ammo and hand grenades, plus our personal weapon, a 45 caliber Thompson sub-machine gun. Our greatest fear was fire. If we took a hit that penetrated our armor, or received a Molotov cocktail (gasoline firebomb) we knew that we had problems. The tank was known as a mobile foxhole or an iron coffin. Our Infantry (foot soldiers) loved our fire-power, but they avoided and stayed away from tanks as they received too much attention. Knowing this, we still had to learn tanks.

Everybody drove the tanks; drivers and assistant drivers were selected and assigned.

The next twenty weeks were an involvement of intensive and arduous training, combining infantry, artillery and tank warfare. We had to learn about our weapons, their cleaning, repairing, correcting malfunctions, and their most effective usage in order to kill.

We stripped and removed cosmoline (protective grease) from all the weapons our government furnished us with. We field stripped and cleaned machine guns and our main and primary weapon—the 75 millimeter (three-inch) artillery piece. We dry ran (practiced) this task until we could accomplish this objective of knowing our weapons. We learned about radio and radio procedures. Our armament consisted of more than just our weapons to kill; we were furnished with allied components such as gyrostabilizers, (used to steady the 75 so it could be fired while the tank was moving). It was fairly accurate, but far from perfect. We had a quadrant (leveling instrument) used for firing on unseen targets (artillery firing); this device gave us our original firing range (distance) after we fired one round. To obtain our horizontal (left-to-right) target we fired and made corrections with our additional instruments, an azimuth indicator; a measuring contrivance similar to a compass used for aligning left-to-right corrections of artillery firing. We had a 30 caliber machine gun mounted to the left of the 75, a telescope and periscope all mounted on and joined adjacent to the 75 gun mount. All of our instruments had to be pinpointed to a given spot, so you could hit what you were looking at when you could actually see your target; everything was being made easy for killing.

Sergeants Sadler and Hartley told us the finer points of tank gunnery. They insisted we follow established procedures and practices, but we were allowed to improvise. When it was time for us to fire our primary weapons, I decided that I would pinpoint and hit the target with 30-caliber fire, noting that every fifth round was a tracer and you could see what your weapon was hitting. After the target was hit with the 30 I would make adjustments or corrections with my aiming devices. This was called putting burst on target, a very effective method in the use of the 75. After continual dry runs (practice), our cadre put us to the test. It was time to select the gunners and to organize the individual tank crews. We were to fire our 75s.

A board was driven into the ground about 1500 yards in front of the tanks on the gunnery range. The portion of board exposed above the ground was the simulated target, or gun emplacement. Our objective and orders were to destroy that board (enemy position). It came my turn to see whether I had learned anything, or was our government wasting the taxpayers' money on me…? I was ordered to fire on the target by my tank commander, Sergeant Hartley. With reluctance and hesitation, I complied. Sergeants Sadler and Hartley, our Cadre instructors, were good—too good. After following my planned procedure I fired an HE (high explosive) round from the 75. I hit the board and cut it in two pieces and knocked it down. That was a mistake—boy was that a mistake! The end result of this booboo was that I was removed from Sergeant Hartley's tank, which was third in the Company line, being the first platoon (composed of five tanks), and placed in the first tank (point tank)—the platoon leader's (officer's) tank—as his gunner.

With this designation I received the first promotion in the company. I was no longer Acting Corporal—I was Full Corporal now, with the power of command. Along with this bullshit I received a ten-dollar raise. My monthly pay went from fifty dollars a month to sixty. Ten dollars extra beer money!

Of course with all that "authority" came responsibility. I was now asked by the officers to bore-sight the 75 when it was their turn to become familiar with this weapon, and to make sure that the officers could save face and hit the target. That wasn't bad—at that time I didn't realize that I was the point—the first tank and lead gun to come under enemy fire. And in Artillery usage of the 75, I was to pinpoint the target. The other four tanks in my platoon aligned up with my firing directions, and when I was on target we laid down a barrage of five guns on target and target area. As far as I was concerned, I was being underpaid. They, meaning the Army, could take that ten bucks and shove it in the appropriate place.

Of course with all the "power and authority of command" there were a few—very few—advantages, and I avoided exercising my "authority" unless they, meaning the Army, caught up with me.

Naturally, during this phase of our training this would occur. We took long marches, both with the tanks and on foot. We made bedrolls and carried our essentials to bivouac (living in the field). Our tent was composed of two shelter halves, made of canvas tenting material, and you teamed up with your buddy. Our bedding was our blanket, our mattress was the ground with a slight cavity dug where your fanny would be so you could lay flat on the ground. You dug a small perimeter around your pup tent so the water would drain away, otherwise the rainwater would seep under your blanket. When the nights got cold, and they did get cold in Louisiana, we would take the tarpaulin covering off our tank and use this by folding it for ground cover and top blanket. Our crew of five would then sleep together to keep warm.

Reveille found you using your pee-pot (metal helmet) as your washbasin. You brushed your teeth, washed and shaved with the use of this protective apparel. In combat when you could not exit your foxhole at night, this container was very convenient for urinating purposes, and thus the name "pee-pot" originated. You consumed your chow from your aluminum mess kit and your hot coffee from your aluminum canteen cup. For your bodily functions or relief you utilized a slit trench. This was a trench usually the width of twelve inches or so. Straddling this trench while squatting, you relieved yourself. For privacy, a fly (canvas fence) encircled the area. By Army directive, these latrines had to be filled and marked after the units finished using them.

This method of schooling or training was effective and very useful. With the minor stresses that were encountered, boys could be separated from the men. Discernment of the leaders, both officers and enlisted men, could be established. Remember, these were the soldiers that were to take and lead the children, or cannon fodder, to war.

This would be the appropriate time to analyze one of our ninety-day wonders (2nd looeys who'd just left Officers Candidate School), the officers that were supposed to lead us. An incident occurred in the field during our training period. Staff Sergeant Sadler climbed to the top of the turret of his tank and asked the 2nd looey, known as "the Penis", what manual (training guide) did he get that crap out of?

First Platoon Sergeant Sadler was broken to Private before sunset. My platoon suffered a great loss. Sadler was a good man, a man you could go to war with. Note—Sadler transferred to the paratroopers and was killed as a participant in D-Day, the invasion of Europe, while the asshole 2nd looey known as "the Penis" got shipped out, probably to a replacement center.

Us kids began to learn what our Army and all of its chicken-shit was all about.

But how could and should a boy cope with it? Conform? Rebel? Or ride along with the tide?

Our destiny was now preordained.

Select units of the Eighth Armored Division were designated as the 710th Tank Battalion on September 20, 1943. We now became C Co., a medium (General Sherman) tank line company of the 710th.

This outfit, now known as "the 710", had to be honed into an effective combat team. This honing or sharpening now went into maximum effort. Training was stepped up, and individual tank crews were united. The process of weeding out the misfits began. The Second and Third Platoons were assigned their permanent second looeys, other looeys we helped train were assigned to other companies in the outfit.

The First Platoon was now led by a Second Lieutenant Harol, a West Point graduate. I was reassigned and ended up as his gunner. This reorganization meant that I was now the lead gunner of the First Platoon—the first tank in the company line of sixteen tanks. I was later to learn that all the shitty and dangerous jobs were delegated to the West Pointer, a good man.

The honing process went into full gear. Forced marches and bivouacs were top priority. In the field we learned tank tactics and how to exist as doughboys or infantry. The Army, through its methods, put weight on the skinny kids, and the fat boys like me took it off. We were hardened by the rigors of our training. Just how effective these Army methods were was shown at an inspection of our woolen olive drab (ODs) winter wearing apparel. Upon entering the service at its reception centers all recruits were properly fitted and attired before being shipped to their designated units. Then I weighed in at 250 fat pounds.

In the sultry heat of a Louisiana summer, during our conversion from boys into so-called soldiers, we would start our day with clean dry fatigues (herringbone twill work clothes); after all of our daily "fun" we would return to the barracks soaked from head to foot with sweat. Salt tablets became a factor in our lives. Getting back to that inspection, the Company Commander looked at me, grabbed the front of my blouse (military jargon for coat) and stated that I was wearing a tent. He wanted to know why I wasn't in proper uniform. After discussion, the CO directed the supply sergeant to obtain the proper attire for me. The Army had sweated sixty-four expensive and expansive pounds of fat from my frame! I was down to my Army weight of 186 pounds.

During our advanced training, I was the assigned gunner of Sergeant Ronald Hartley's tank. Hartley, our Cadre, was an excellent instructor, the perfect soldier, a man you could go to war with. I, and the first platoon, were being denied that privilege. The CO and the selected cadre were pulled out of the 710 to train others. We, of the First Platoon, lost a darn good man.

The Battalion was reorganized and its roster was brought up to date. Changes were made, the Cadre left, promotions were posted.

Our newly activated 710 was under the command of a Major, composed of: Headquarters Company; the line or fighting companies ABC, with General Sherman (medium) tanks; D Company, with light tanks; and the Service Company.

My unit, C Co., its Commander, Officers and line of march, were as follows: Captain Richard, Company Commander; Lieutenants Harol, First Platoon; Gavlik, Second Platoon; Caffin, Third Platoon; and a Maintenance Officer. The First Platoon Buck Sergeant Karle was back-up tank behind Lt. Harol. Staff Sergeant Brier, Platoon Sergeant; Buck Sergeant Alvin; and fifth in line, Buck Sergeant Floyd; followed by the Second Platoon with five tanks; the Third Platoon with its five and the CO's tank in the rear. The commissioned officers and/or the sergeants were in charge of and responsible for a tank and its crew.

The process of the United States Army indoctrination of kids or boys into becoming tankers was stipulated by Army Training Manuals.

Our sweet innocent boys undertook forced marches on foot, lived like animals in the field, conquered obstacle courses, crawled under barb wire while live 30 caliber machine-gun bullets were being fired overhead, sampled chemical warfare while being exposed to tear gas, and became familiar with and/or used to all the weapons of war. We learned how to effectively use these weapons to kill or destroy, including firing 50 caliber machine guns at flying model airplanes. Our favorite expression at this time, the corruption of our youthful lives, was, "Boy, this is hell!" How wrong we were: *hell was yet to come.*

3: Specialized Training—Amphibious

January 10, 1944 found us on a military train sleeping in Pullman cars; headed for the Marine Base at San Diego, California. For a month we lived in pyramidal tents erected on the base parade grounds. Marine Combat Veterans attempted to cram knowledge obtained from their experiences into our, the dogies (Army soldiers'), heads. We climbed and descended cargo nets from wooden barriers and finally from a ship bouncing in the ocean turbulence into LCM (Landing Craft, Men—an open craft with a ramp in front) training as foot soldiers. During this phase of our amphibious training we embarked aboard a LCI (Landing Craft, Infantry) a continuation of our infantry training. A notable experience or event occurred: about 100 yards in the left front of our LCI a submarine (US) popped out of the surface of the Pacific Ocean and landed on its belly. Apparently our Navy was having a shakedown cruise of a new sub and crew.

During our cruise we encountered swells (massive waves of water); we were getting our sea-legs and were of course seasick.

Our cruise was effective; we "conquered" San Clemente Island sixty-five miles off the California coast on foot as Infantry. Apparently we didn't do it right, because we boarded an LST (Landing Ship, Tank) and reconquered San Clemente two more times as Tankers with our tanks. One was a daytime landing, the other a night landing. Upon embarkation from this cruise, our new destination was a landing with tanks at Avila Bay, California. From there we reported to Camp San Luis Obispo, February 19, 1944. We never returned to the Marine Base at San Diego. We had our taste of sea duty; the chow was good, the living conditions excellent.

San Luis Obispo, an Army Camp nestled in the Cherro Valley at the foot of Santa Lucia Mountains of the Coast Range midway between Los Angeles and San Francisco, became our next home away from home. We lived and existed in wooden hutments that would accommodate six, but in our situation these hutments were occupied by one tank crew.

Even though it was the rainy season, I've enjoyed the snow in California. The scenery and the country was beautiful and our conditions were decent. Here we were attached to the 81st Infantry Division. The 81st Infantry Division, commanded by Major General Paul J. Mueller, US Army, had received exceptionally thorough training. Nicknamed the "Wildcat Division" and wearing a reproduction of this feline as a shoulder patch, it had trained for two years and three months, participated in extensive maneuvers in Alabama, Tennessee and in the California and Arizona deserts. Upon being designated for island operations in the Pacific, they had been taken in hand by the Amphibious Training Command, Pacific Fleet, for this mission.

The 81st showed us the importance of the Infantry with its close proximity and the individual firepower of the foot soldier. This close relationship protected our tanks from the rear, especially in the type of jungle warfare we would encounter in the Pacific Theater of operations. The tanks in turn had the armament and firepower to knock out any hot spots the infantry ran into. This was a Tank-Infantry Team, and it was very effective.

The intensive and stepped-up training of early 1943 eased. I guess headquarters figured we were ready and they were going to make us earn our pay, such as it was. The Army's philosophy is that idle hands create mischief, so they have a great number of activities scheduled for you. To get us out of the company area, Lt. Harol took us out for walks, not marches, into the rolling hills of the Santa Lucia Mountains. There we enjoyed the beauty of California. We smoked when we wanted to, and had informal bull sessions on any subject; very little if any pertained to the military. You could see that Lt. Harol was not, I repeat, was not a ninety-day wonder second looey. He was a different breed, a West Pointer.

In March and April of 1944, the men—no longer boys—of the 710th received their last furlough. We left one of the nicer of our Army homes, Obispo, on April 25 by Army convoy taking our tanks and gear to our new base, Camp Cooke. Camp Cooke, California, was a typical Army wartime training base, windswept, arid and desolate. Here we reacquainted ourselves with our weapons, firing them for the last time Stateside. We then learned how to waterproof our tanks and other vehicles.

Finally the day arrived; we had to clean the tanks and our weaponry, and turn these back to the US Army Ordinance so they could be of use in training the next outfit of tankers. Then came the "showdown" inspections. Our woolen olive drab winter wearing apparel was turned in and overseas clothing was issued; our excess belongings, those which would be of no use, were sent to our civilian homes.

In June 1944 we marched out, lugging our barracks bags to the troop train. The overseas procedures started to take form. For the first time in our Army "careers" we were ordered to remove and gladly took off the nuisance known as the necktie. Aboard our troop train we enjoyed the scenic beauty of the western coast of the United States. This enjoyable trip began in California, continued through Oregon and then on to the state of Washington. At the very northwestern tip of this beautiful state, Seattle and Fort Lawton was our port of embarkation.

Final processing took place for the next four days. We received our overseas "physicals" and took care of the paperwork involved with overseas troop movements. The Army at this particular time would not and did not trust us. Passes were not issued, so we had to observe the city of Seattle from our base on the hill overlooking that fine place.

4: Hawaii—Jungle Training

Being young and indoctrinated by the American system and the motion picture industry, I looked forward to our cruise, hopefully on a pleasure boat, to our unknown destination.

On June 14, 1944 at 1800 hours (6 P.M.) the Battalion boarded our "love boat", the USS *Cape Cod*—a banana boat, converted to a wartime troopship. This "luxury ocean liner" had troop berthing, pipe-racks with canvas tied to the pipe, stacked five high in the cargo holds of the ship. We existed on breakfast and dinner chow—which would prevail in all of our seafaring excursions. Lunch was eliminated. Our "heads" (toilet facilities) were an open trough with a continual stream of salt water slushing and forcing the excretions into the ocean. A shower was something you dreamed of. The stench and odors in the hold became unbearable.

After forty-eight hours at sea we were told our destination, the island of Oahu, home of Pearl Harbor and Schofield Barracks in the Hawaiian Islands. This cruise lasted eight days. June 22 we rounded Diamond Head and docked in the harbor of the port of Honolulu. The traditional Hawaiian welcome of the native Wahine women, in their grass sarongs and halters with their leis, were missing. We were not even honored with a band welcoming us to this tropical paradise. That was typical of the US Army—forgetting the niceties of life.

Our next mode of transportation was a miniature train with open cars that were used to haul sugar cane and pineapples. Our route was in the valleys of the mountain ranges, where many man-made caves with the storage of man's implements of war were highly visible. Our destination was Schofield Barracks, a permanent Army installation.

At Schofield you could sense, and knew, that something was brewing. We undertook a most concentrated training period at the Unit Jungle Training Center. They crammed us with the use and application of all forms of demolitions, shape, plastic, cordite and satchel charges (thirty pounds of dynamite enclosed in canvas satchels). One thing of interest occurred during this phase of training. The Jungle Training Unit was located in the jungle area of the island of Oahu, a mountainous area with jungle growth of bamboo and banyan trees with a large stream of fresh water. Our schooling included the exploding of the demolition charges and the after-effects of these explosions. With these continual explosions in the mountainous altitude we would get wet from a series of sun-and-showers, and then the warmth of the Hawaiian sun would dry us. Of course with these sun-and-showers came the glorious rainbows. The end of a rainbow descended about 100 feet in front of my buddy Lightning (Forest Kern) and myself. Both of us with dreams and visions of wealth, sought out our "pot of gold". No luck; we did not find any spending money. It took me years to realize that the "pot of gold" was the island of Oahu, our Pacific Paradise... so, I can still dream.

Our training included how to survive and exist in the jungle. We learned that the food that the monkeys ate, we could eat too. We developed the skills and know-how of judo, how to kill with your hands. Two steel cables were suspended across the stream. We were to ford the stream with and by the use of these bouncing cables. I fell off the cable into the stream and got to the opposite shore the easy way: I swam. Another test of wit and endurance was the obstacle course. We were issued M-1 rifles, the Infantry's weapon, with very dull bayonets, and directed to run this course consisting of barbed wire strung close to the ground in a given area. We were directed to emerge on the opposite side of this field of wire, the Army way, that was to slide on your back while using your weapon to elevate the wire so you would not get hung up on the barbs. If you crept on your stomach you would get stuck on the barbed wire. After your successful emergence and victory over this obstacle you now faced the enemy; bags stuffed with straw. You were to stab this enemy with your bayonet. While I was sticking the foe with my bayonet, I was slammed in the back with a partially filled sandbag and knocked for a loop. Upon arising I followed the rope which had the sand bag attached to a branch of the tree, and sitting on this branch was a GI laughing his head off; he controlled this device on a pendulum principle. I retrieved my weapon and proceeded to hack away at the rope with my bayonet. It wasn't my day. I was not successful in my efforts. The GI up the tree cursed at me, but his sandbag was still attached to his rope, so he could conquer another victim.

Another unique experience concerned the second looey known as "the Phoney", the "gangster" who, while in the States training, was the braggart who was going to "wipe out a thousand Japs with his machine gun". This officer led the Company on a night jungle march with the use of a compass. He was to lead the Company through the jungle of banyan trees to a specified destination on the opposite side. When we started out, the jungle was pitch dark, and the meager light from the moon and sky could not penetrate the darkness and thick foliage. A banyan tree has large roots growing above ground, and during our compass course exercise we found that by looking up we could see the sky. We climbed to the top of the trees and could see the jungle expanse below us. This tree-top expedition was understandable. The next obstruction we encountered was a small creek about eight feet wide. The looey, not knowing how to swim, and fearing the water, believing that still water runs deep, ordered his tank driver to enter the water and lead us across. I wonder if the looey thought that if he led and went under the water that nobody in the company would save him from drowning; then again, maybe nobody would save him—they would let him drown. We waded across the creek, a lot of wet fatigues but no drowning, and we were now in a reasonably clear area out of the jungle. The looey, even with the use of his compass and the military map, led the company in the wrong direction; we were lost. After stumbling around in the dark for hours, somebody who could read a map and use a compass took charge. We finally located our designated position and rendezvoused with the Company Commander. Nothing was said, no inquiries or explanations were asked for in front of the enlisted men.

This officer, our leader, the one to take us into combat, showed his fear, got us lost, misused and abused his position of command.

Was this an omen of things to come?

5: Hawaii—Combat Loading

We got our jungle training behind us. The most memorable imprint of this Hawaiian "vacation" was our journey from Schofield Barracks, on the windward side of the island of Oahu, up the Koolau Mountain Range, which dissects two-thirds of the island. We drove a road known as the Pali Highway, which rises on a gentle incline as you progress from the windward to the leeward side of the island. The temperature drops and you have a gentle breeze from the trade winds; mother nature air-conditions this highway. After enjoying the temperature and the clean, lush environment you come to the end of the highway and encounter a precipice, with a vertical drop straight down 150 feet, more or less. The highest rise of the Koolau Mountain Range with its precipice overlooks the Kaneohe Valley. There is an area reserved for stopping your vehicle and enjoying the scenic beauty.

The eruptions of the volcanoes on the floor of the Pacific Ocean issued streams of molten rock. This rock solidified into grotesque shapes and forms. The turbulence of the ocean washed soil onto this solidified rock. Birds, through droppings etc., deposited seeds onto the soil. The tropical heat, moisture and ideal growing conditions suited the seeds; they flourished, died, decomposed and created rich, fertile soil. With the help of God, the island of Oahu was created, enriching mankind. Of course there are exceptions. Mother nature can and has given Man paradise; nature has also given us purgatory in the Pacific Islands.

Back to the Koolau Mountain Range on the Hawaiian island of Oahu. The end of the Pali Highway and its precipice bring Man to nature at its best at the Nuvanu Pali Lookout. You oversee miles of cultivated flora, the white sands of the beach with the gentle waves of water from the blue Pacific Ocean rolling in. The quiet, the beauty of the scenery and the cool trade winds—truly, it's heaven on earth.

To the left, as you faced the ocean of the Lookout Point, was a massive boulder protruding skyward. A parachute was stuck to this formation. The word was that it was a Japanese parachute from the sneak December 7, 1941 attack on our Naval Base at Pearl Harbor and on other military establishments located on the island. (I believe it was staged for propaganda purposes.)

You are at the top of the precipice, your destination is in the Kaneohe Valley. How do you get there? Our company truck driver, Moose, loaded us aboard the truck, directed us to hang on—shifted the truck to its lowest gearing and proceeded down. A roadway of curves and s-bends was blasted out of the volcanic rock. With slow and careful manipulation of the vehicle you descended to the floor of the Kanehoe Valley. You then released your hold; you did not have to hang on any more. (The irony of this wonderful experience of the Pali System is being denied to the unknowledgeable tourist—modern man, demanding speed, has built a tunnel system, eliminating the highlights.)

Back to the matter in hand—the confrontation with the Japanese Empire—*the War*.

On July 11, 1944, our outfit was relocated to Fort Hase, a wartime camp situated in the Kanehoe Valley region. Everything was stepped up; the push was on. We were furnished with new tanks, armament and equipment needed to go to war. Everybody was tense. We were faced with the fears of war and the unknown. This fear and pressure caught up with some and was noticeably apparent. The 3rd Platoon Sergeant, to mask his fear, became totally obnoxious. My crew and I being of the 1st Platoon began to receive the brunt of his shit. I took this Staff Sergeant aside and told him, "Boy, cut the shit, remember we are going to war!"

This Sergeant could not cope with his fears; he was removed from being Platoon Sergeant and leadership, and reassigned as the Company Armorer, a non-leadership job. Another who couldn't apparently cut the mustard was a gunner of the 2nd Platoon looey's tank. He suffered a wound; accidentally shot himself in the knee with a 45 caliber hand weapon. My assistant was promoted and made gunner of the 2nd Platoon looey's tank.

Final organization started shaping up. We, being consumers of alcoholic stimulants, but whose budget would only allow beer, named our new mode of transportation—a 32 ton General Sherman Tank—"Champagne". It's compliment was: Tank Commander, Lieutenant Harol; Driver, T/4 (Technician 4th Grade) Williams; Gunner, Corporal Ed Luzinas; Assistant Gunner, T/5 Oliver; Assistant Driver, PFC Harken. T/5 Oliver, a very good man, came in as a replacement for my assistant who was promoted.

Now we had to prepare our equipment and ourselves to be fit to go to war and earn our "pay" from our Government. It began with the removal of the protective cosmoline from our new weapons. Whole crews pitched in and worked together toward this accomplishment. Then the drivers and their assistants checked the new tanks until they were satisfied that the tank met with their approval. The gunners and their helpers checked the firing components, sighting devices, checked and made final adjustments to the machine guns so they would not jam while firing. They bore-sighted the 75s and aligned the periscopes with the 75s bore sight so the gunners could hit what they were looking at. They secured extra periscopes and spare parts for both weaponry and electrical systems. We tested radio transmitters and receivers, and obtained extra parts. We checked and rechecked, hoping that we did everything that we could possibly do or think of doing to give us a feeling of some degree of security, knowing that the lives of our tank crew, our buddies, might be affected.

While all this activity was occurring, the tank gunners received orders to mount our 50 caliber machine guns atop the tanks' turret and stand by, as a Japanese air raid was anticipated. The gunners made note that we did not have any 50 caliber munitions—we were told that it would be brought to us. False alarm—no raid.

We then continued on with our preparations to go to war. Naval reconnaissance showed that the landing from our Landing Ship, Tanks (LSTs) would not be beached and when vacating the LSTs our tanks would be partially submerged under water. That meant tank breathing (snorkel) tunnels or shafts had to be welded on and behind the engine compartment. Welders worked around the clock to accomplish this. The purpose and intention of these vertical shafts was to allow our engines to receive air necessary for the combustion of its fuel/gasoline. One snorkel served this purpose, the other was for the exhaust of the gases. Both had to rise above the ocean level or the waters would flood the engine compartment and drown your engine. Then the tank or vehicle would be disabled—dead in the water and blocking other vehicles exiting from the landing ramp of the LST.

The Ordnance Trucks then arrived loaded with munitions. The required and desired ammunition was stored in every nook and cranny. A great amount of time and thought was devoted to these preliminary preparations. It had to be during working hours, as time that the Army allowed for rest was used for that purpose, rest; we were so tired and pooped that the moment we lay down, we slept. Okay, we earned our "pay", we fulfilled our obligations. The tanks furnished to us by our Government were combat ready, we hoped.

Now we had to think and provide for ourselves. We knew our grateful Government would furnish us with canned beans, canned hash and so on. They also provide us with heavily waxed boxes containing hard chocolate, cigarettes, cheese and dry concoctions. One of these, when and if dissolved in water, became coffee, another became a lemon drink... The Army's intentions were good, all of the above would sustain life, but it was still crap. We had dreams of providing our tank, Champagne, and its crew with goodies. Opportunities would knock. Our capable, highly trained and skillful crew would open the door for the opportunities that would present themselves at the Naval Base known as Pearl Harbor. Thanks to our Government, the skills and daring of our scrounges and the expediting of our crew to the Naval Stores warehoused at Pearl, we did obtain a supply of "goodies", the necessities of our youthful existence. The process of the combat loading of our LST began. Our LST docked at the submarine pen area of and in Pearl Harbor.

December 7, 1941, the armed forces of the Japanese nation bombed Pearl Harbor. Judge the facts and form your own opinions.

The week of August 1 to August 8, 1944, was the history of our involvement with Pearl Harbor. We of the Army sweated and accomplished everything that was stipulated by the top echelon and high brass. It was now the Navy's responsibility. All loading procedures and every involvement with Pearl was begun and worked on in the darkest hours of the day. Our loading area was illuminated by artificial lighting. Conditions were ideal for our scrounger. He could locate Naval Stores and appropriated a case of canned pineapple. Opportunity was knocking, so we opened the door. A detail from the crew liberated an additional case of pineapple and two cases of spam from the Naval Warehouse. Our scrounger had a good night. Champagne's crew was now enriched with two cases of pineapple and two cases of spam. These were stored on the interior deck in the turret, underneath the 30 caliber machine gun and the 75. Knowing the ways and methods of the Army, our crew could not release news of our escapade. The Army did not, I repeat did not, have any scruples concerning the involvement of goodies; they would "appropriate" ours.

The loading of the LST took shape. To the rear of the interior well of the LST, equipment of and for a field hospital was stored. Next came our Company field kitchen, headquarters detailing and equipment. Then came our tanks, all backed in the load well of the LST in the reverse order of departure—the five tanks of the third platoon backed in first, the next five tanks, the second platoon followed, and finally the first platoon, with Lieutenant Harol's tank, Champagne, loaded last, being the first tank to exit.

6: En route—Destination Unknown

Topside, in front of the ship's command or bridge area and officers' quarters, 55-gallon drums containing fuel were stacked and secured so they would not roll around on the deck in foul weather. A small observation airplane was part of the combat cargo. In addition to war supplies, numerous refrigeration units were used for storage of food for the participants of this great production; war.

On August 8, 1944, carrying only the necessities, a musette bag with toiletries, change of underwear and socks, our Thompson submachine gun, a bedroll with our shelter half and blanket, we boarded our LST. This was to be our home for the next forty days. Our duffel bags containing our possessions were stored and would catch up to us. We were now under the command and jurisdiction of the United States Navy. Their job: to transport us and land us safely at a destination which was unknown to us at this time.

We were now about to get a taste, which proved to be an enjoyable taste, of how the other half—the Navy—existed. Before we got underway to leave Pearl Harbor, we were ordered to go below to our living quarters and stay there until commanded otherwise. Our loading and other preparations were accomplished in darkness. We would not be allowed to see Pearl Harbor in daylight as we left our staging area of embarkation.

It was quite apparent that the wheels—High Command—did not want us, the cannon fodder, to witness the wanton wreak of Pearl Harbor. As young men willing to give our lives for our country, the "wheels" were denying us our freedom of choice.

I do not believe that the vision and knowledge of the carnage of Pearl Harbor would have demoralized us. This conjecture shall be left to the reader.

An LST, landing ship, tank, is a ship designed and built for amphibious warfare. The bow or front of the ship has doors that open to the right and left. A ramp is then dropped, forming a roadway, and vehicles exit on this ramp. It has the facilities required for troop transport: good chow, ample living quarters with clean bedding, and heads with real toilets and showers. The Navy had access to good edible rations and the preparation of these rations was excellent. It promised to be a good trip. I always did state that if I could swim as far as I could walk I would join the Navy. Our duties were light, gunners stood watch, cooks helped prepare rations, others helped with chores under supervision. The Army did not chip paint.

We even had our own swimming pool... The bow doors leaked, allowing water in the area between the bow and the ramp. The ramp was leak-proof and prevented the salt water from entering the cargo well. We cooled off there. Fresh water was limited, and its use restricted. Whenever we encountered rain squalls we took a freshwater bath. Our Navy personnel told us how and allowed us the use of their lines (ropes) to tie our dirty fatigues and drop them over the side of the ship, and the water acted as a washing machine to wash our clothes. The sun then dried them. For recreation we would go to the bow of the ship and enjoy the roller-coaster effect of the ocean swells and waves. A few, not many, took seasick; that was part of the game.

When the smoking lamp was lit we could smoke in the rear (fantail) of the ship. All other areas topside were restricted from smoking or any exposed fire because of the storage of the 55-gallon drums of gasoline. The fantail was our favorite gathering place. Here we could smoke, straighten out our thoughts and shoot the bull. After a great deal of bragging, dreaming and speculating about the opposite gender, we got down to the matter at hand: our destination and our destiny.

The strategist of our gathering stated that the Allied Forces had assaulted and captured Guadalcanal, in the Solomon Island chain, in August 1942. We now had a staging area to aid further island conquests. In January 1943, Australian troops defeated the Japanese in Papua, New Guinea, the south-west Pacific area.

The Allies—Americans—had defeated the Japanese at Guadalcanal; the Australians were victorious in Papua. These losses by the Japanese had shown that the Japanese were not invincible at sea, in the air, or in the jungle. The Allied Forces had now stopped the future conquests by the Japanese. Our Navy then enjoyed the strategic victory at Midway. Our Marines established a staging area in the Solomon Islands. Our nation had time to mobilize. Production was at full wartime capacity. The waiting was over; the Allied drive from fortified island to fortified island had begun. This was known as "the Atoll War".

The next scheduled onslaught was Tarawa—an Atoll in the Gilbert Islands. The objective was to establish a base or staging area near Hong Kong, and from this base launch an invasion of Japan. We captured Kwajalen, the largest coral atoll in the Marshall Islands. The next island, Eniwetok, 670 miles from Truk, the great Japanese stronghold in the Pacific, was taken in one day in a simple invasion, inexpensive of lives. In June of 1944, the Marines and the Army's 27th Division, with support units, had their work cut out for them. They were ordered to seize Saipan, Tinian and Guam, islands of the Mariana Group. The occupation by the Allies of these key strongholds of the Japanese defensive chain would cut the Japanese supply lines and isolate Truk, Guam and Saipan, which would furnish the Allies with advanced air and naval bases. It opened the options of hitting the Philippines, Formosa (now known as Taiwan) or Okinawa. Many other islands and atolls were never invaded. They were leapfrogged, left to wither and die, and were neutralized by air strikes from time to time.

The military "genius" of our bull sessions decreed that Truk, the Gibraltar of the Pacific, was to be our objective. Okay, we decided that our job was Truk, so we went back to enjoying our cruise; being firm believers in what is to be is to be—the book is written and Fate is the author. Smoking and watching the screws (propellers that drove the ship) churn up the phosphorus of the ocean, while we were in the fantail area, gave us time to think and analyze our situation. Our analysis of our situation did not appear promising; it gave us nothing to look forward to.

On a sunny August day, the routine of shipboard living was broken up. We crossed the equator. At a ceremony which was purely for kicks and entertainment, King Neptune transformed us, the Army Gis, from landlubbers to pollywogs to trusted shellbacks. We had crossed the equator. But as in life a price had to be paid. While sliding down a greased board, my right leg encountered a metal tie-down, welded to the deck, which was used to secure cargo. The tie-down would not budge, my right ankle did—result, sprained ankle and immense pain. I hobbled below to our living quarters and passed out. A great amount of chaos ensued. I came to, was assisted into a lower sack and made as comfortable as conditions allowed. The ship's Medic attended me and notified me that he would recommend to the skipper of the ship that I should be examined by a doctor ashore.

On the twenty-fourth day of August we anchored at Guadalcanal as part of our amphibious training. Dry runs (practice landings) were made and we were fine-tuned for the impending operation. The Navy strapped me into a wire litter and lowered me over the side of our LST into a LCM (landing craft, men) which then proceeded to shore. I was taken to the Field Hospital. After examination and X-rays, the doctor recommended that I remain there for treatment and not go into combat. After consideration, being young, naive and instilled with the gung-ho spirit, I made another stupid blunder: I requested that I be returned to my outfit. The doctor then gave me sedatives and recommended that I avoid using my right leg. The medicine would alleviate the pain. Rest and time would allow me usage of my leg while being careful.

The guys relocated my sack closer to the head. The Navy improvised a crutch and allowed me its use. My buddy, good old Forest "Lightning" Kern, of Scranton Pa., came through again. During basic training in the field at a bivouac I had been sick with heat prostration. The CO sent me back to the Battalion medics. Our Doctor directed me to take salt tablets, go to the barracks and rest. I was cold—summertime in Louisiana and cold! I was awaken by my buddy, Lightning, in the barracks. He said that I was shivering and he covered me with his blanket. Lightning told me that he came in from the field to make sure that I was all right. I pass out in Louisiana, I pass out aboard an LST—and Lightning is there to help out! My tank crew checked on me daily. Lightning made sure that I got fed. He brought me the meals personally. He kept me informed of the goings-on aboard. Our whistle-happy First Sergeant came to see if I was fit for duty and ordered me to shave. Lightning shaved me. This is what is known as the buddy system. Lightning helped make unbearable situations bearable. There shall be a great deal more about Lightning.

Normal shipboard life resumed. Our routine was broken up with the refueling of a PT Boat. The PT Boat docked alongside of us at sea and fuel from our LST was pumped into the Torpedo Boat's storage tanks. The smoking lamp was out during refueling.

August 26, 1944, found us in the Solomon Island Group at Florida Island. We were anchored in the waters known as Iron Bottom Sound. A Navy swimmer diving under water reported that numerous sunken ships were present in our vicinity, and the ocean floor was strewn with wreckage. A large manta ray, (devilfish) estimated at six to eight feet long, wingtip to wingtip, took up residence next to our ship, scavenging the garbage from our meals. We departed the Solomon Islands. At sea, we learned our objective and destination.

7: Destination Known—The Palau Islands

The Palaus were the most powerful and the most strategically placed strongholds of the Japanese Empire. Following the fall of the Marianas they, the Palaus, were on the flank of any attack on the Philippine Islands from the south-east, 450 miles from Mindanao. The Palaus are the westernmost of the Caroline Islands. The western Carolines contained three desired targets: Ulithi, a large atoll with a deep and extensive lagoon which would provide a fine fleet anchorage; Yap, an airbase made up of four small islands; and the larger group of islands known as the Palaus. As we, CCo., 710 Tank Battalion, were participants in the seizure of Angaur and Peleliu, we shall spotlight and deal in detail with these two islands of the Palau Chain.

The Palau Group of islands lies at the farthest end of the vast Caroline Islands chain, just north of the equator, westward from the Gilbert and Marshall Islands, to within 500 miles of the southern Philippines. The Palaus, along with other islands of the Carolines, Marianas, Marshalls and Gilbert Islands are referred to as being part of Micronesia—literally, "tiny islands".

The Palaus were initially discovered and annexed by Spain in 1543. Spain made little effort to administer or develop the islands. Spain sold the islands to Germany in 1899. German exploitation developed economic possibilities in the islands. In October 1914, the Japanese nation took control of German possessions in Micronesia. The League of Nations mandate granted the Japanese nation the possessions of the Germans in Micronesia, thereby legitimizing the Japanese seizure in 1920. Japan withdrew from the League of Nations in 1935. Japan's title to all former German Pacific Colonies north of the equator went undisputed until that certain morning in the month of September in the year 1944. There were two reasons for taking the Palaus. The first, to remove a definite threat to General MacArthur's flank in his progress to the Philippines. The second, to secure a base to support his operation. A directive, code-named "Stalemate 11" was issued by Fleet Admiral Chester W. Nimitz, Commander-in-Chief Pacific Ocean Areas (CINCPOA). It called for the invasion of the Southern Palaus on September 15 (September 14—west-46 longitude time) by the following forces:

1st—Peleliu Landing Group: 1st Marine Division commanded by Major General William H. Rupertus of The First "The Old Breed" Marines veterans of Guadalcanal and Cape Gloucester on New Britain Island.

2nd—Angaur Attack and Landing Force: 81st Infantry Division commanded by Major General Paul J. Mueller, US Army nicknamed "the Wildcat Division", unbloodied, yet to receive its baptism of fire, but receiving thorough training topped off by amphibious landing rehearsals in Hawaii and on Guadalcanal.

The Japanese Imperial Headquarters ordered Lieutenant General Sadae Inoue to hold the Palau Islands at all costs. The Commander of the Palaus Sector Group—Lieutenant General Sadae Inoue—was also Commanding General of the 14th Division Imperial Japanese Army, one of the oldest and best units of the Japanese Armed Forces, with a history dating back to the Sino-Japanese War (1894–1895) and an outstanding record in the Russo-Japanese War (1904–1905). The 14th's Regiments of Infantry were the 2nd, 15th and the 59th, the 53rd Independent Mixed Brigade and a miscellany of smaller units, giving support for combatants and construction. The greater portion of General Inoue's force, estimated upward of 25,000, were on the big island of Babelthaup, to the north of Peleliu and Angaur islands. General Inoue's forces were known to have had special training to counter landing operations. The potential of Japanese reinforcements of the Peleliu and Angaur garrisons was real, and had to be considered and dealt with. Intelligence reported that the large island of the Palau Group, Babelthaup, twenty miles long and five miles wide, was heavily fortified and garrisoned. Attempts to capture Babelthaup could result in a bloodbath like the Tarawa Campaign. The terrain of Babelthaup was the rugged results of submarine volcanic action, limiting the possibility of airfield construction. The decision was made to simply neutralize it and the other major islands, and to seize the three most southerly islands, Peleliu, Ngesebus and Angaur. Troops that were scheduled to take Babelthaup would be used to take the islands of Yap and Ulithi.

8: Commanders and Planning

The Palau Islands stood as one of the key strongholds in Japan's second line of defense. In early 1944, Japan's first line of defense, New Guinea and the Marshall Islands, were eliminated, and the Central Caroline Islands has been bypassed and neutralized.

Back to the 710th Tank Battalion: our destiny was approaching. Our orders were that, along with the 81st Infantry, we were to be the First Marine Division's floating reserve, if called upon to assist the Marines on Peleliu. If the First Marines deemed that our assistance was unnecessary, our assignment was to take and secure the island of Angaur, eight miles south of Peleliu.

My ankle was coming along nicely, but time was running out. I had to obtain some degree of mobility. We cut a canvas legging in half. Lacing the legging tight, it became a brace and support for the ankle. Far from perfect, but it had to do. Now to learn to walk again. Returning to our favorite gathering place, the ship's fantail, the discussions were all directed to the new turn of events; the Palaus. We were grateful it was not the island of Truk. Truk, being a Japanese stronghold, was to be bypassed and left to whither on the vine and die. After counting our blessings that it was not Truk, we began to assess our situation. We were awed by the size of the convoy that our Navy furnished us with. There were flat-tops (aircraft carriers), battle wagons, cruisers and destroyer escorts, which circled our convoy continuously in search of enemy submarines. Included in the convoy was a flotilla of amphibious ships and the large troop carriers that transported the foot soldiers.

The logistics and planning necessary for an expedition of this size were kicked around. It was noted that not only the tools and weapons of war had to be considered, but also the troops, the force that was to hit the beach, secure a foothold and finally seize a fortified enemy stronghold, a small island where reinforcements could easily be dispersed to troubled areas. Once the foot soldier hits the beach, he is on his own. The Navy and its fighter aircraft can be called upon for support in places of heavy resistance, but the foot soldier is strictly on his own until the beachhead is secured. The wounded are treated by medics assigned to each unit and, if possible, stretcher-bearers would carry the wounded to the beach area. The dead were left for graves registration units.

When the infantry has secured a foothold on the beach, support units, including engineers to clear obstacles and make roadways, tanks and artillery are landed, to assist the infantry. A signals corps has to be set up to provide communications. Munitions, food, water and a thousand and one details have to be provided and accounted for. Aid stations have to be established to care for the sick and wounded. Hospital ships have to be available for the treatment of the more seriously wounded. Air evacuation has to be provided to take the wounded to base hospitals. Knowing all the planning and detailing involved in an invasion of islands held by enemy forces, and that if there are wounded men, all activity ceases until the wounded are tended to and cared for, gave us a little sense of confidence.

Angaur and Peleliu were small island secretively and heavily fortified; reinforcements were easily dispersed to troubled areas. The Infantry in the first wave to hit the beach have their work and many problems cut out (and usually spelled out) for them. The infantryman's job is to secure a good foothold on the beach, then move inland. While his is undertaking this assignment, he, the foot soldier, is on his own. He calls upon naval guns and air fighter fire support when he encounters heavy resistance. Prior to the first wave's landing, the beach receives a preliminary and a terrific bombardment from naval guns and aircraft. When the Navy fires a broadside with its 16 inch guns you wonder why the island doesn't sink! Until the Infantry secures the beachhead so that support units can land and do their assigned jobs, the first wave is on its own.

That is the insight and training we received from Marine Combat Veterans at San Diego. The Marines were also very emphatic: do not run over the dead Japs with our tanks, the stench of rotting human flesh would nauseate us.

Our time was getting near at hand. We would not only experience, but we would have to live with this experience, *war*, the rest of our natural lives.

We were assigned our job. Final preparations were undertaken with the hopes of a successful completion of our mission. Checks and rechecks of equipment and procedures were conducted, until we felt satisfied that all that could be accomplished on our level was accomplished. Military Intelligence detailing information about Peleliu and Angaur was unclear. Jungle growth of weeds and vegetation concealed General Inoue's defenses. This growth prevented aerial reconnaissance from obtaining the approximate height and disposition of the terrain. Cliffs, eaves and defiles were not revealed to the camera's eye.

The photographic reconnaissance was incomplete and unsatisfactory. In July and August, Navy and Army aircraft took both vertical and oblique photos. The USS *Seawolf*, a submarine, took photographs of all possible landing beaches. This material gave our forces a workable map, though not entirely adequate. A target area grid system was superimposed. Aerial photograph interpreters spotted many ground installations. The map showed the southern part of Peleliu to be low and flat. The airfield was a good one, with both fighter and bomber strips of hard-packed coral.

North of the airfield were the utility installations, aircraft hangars, troop barracks, power plants, the radio station, water reservoirs and administration buildings. Just behind these installations appeared to be rising ground well masked by jungle growth and vegetation. The First Marine Division planners knew that this area north of the airfield was the key terrain feature of the available map. The vegetation had the contours. No defensive installations were revealed by aerial observations.

The map finally drawn up indicated the high ground to be a continuous ridge system flanked by a good road on either side. The ground flattened out briefly, and the east road angled through a wide draw to converge with the west road. Inland, a narrower ridge and several more hills were noted.

The planners had to be content with guesses; it was impossible to send patrols ashore on an island so small and so strongly held.

The Navy's Underwater Demolition Teams (UDTs) scouted approaches to the beaches, destroyed obstacles and mines and reported reef conditions.

On Peleliu, there was no dearth of wide sandy beaches suitable for landing operations. Four sets of beaches were taken into consideration.

Beach Purple presented the greatest natural advantages. This was no more than 200 yards wide, and it appeared impractical to bring ships as large as LSTs directly to the beach. However, this was equally obvious to the Japanese, and they had set up their strongest defensive weapons and methods here.

A projected landing on Scarlet Beach was discarded. Beach Amber lay along the north-western peninsula where the reef was the widest. Inland of the beach, a level shelf was dominated by high ground at ranges of 100–300 yards. A successful landing here would place key terrain in the Division's hands. But failure to capture the ridge line would leave our forces on low ground, without room to maneuver, with the enemy looking down their throats.

A landing on the White and Orange beaches, followed by a drive straight across the island, would seize the airfield and divide the defenders. The officers who were about to participate in this operation, and did so, were unanimous that this course, the chosen one, was the best one.

Navy Carrier Task Forces began the softening-up process of the Palaus. They attacked the islands as early as March 30 and again in July and August. Long-range bombers from General McArthur's area, planes of the Army's Fifth Air Force stations in New Guinea, struck frequently at the Palaus in support of the Marianas invasion bombers of the Thirteenth Air Force from New Guinea and the Admiralties, and pounded the islands. Hundreds of tons of bombs rained down on the Japanese, but General Inoue's helpless troops remained secure in their underground tunnels and caves. The Army Air Force had dropped over 600 tons of bomb in nine sorties. Most of General Inoue's buildings and installation above ground were demolished. The airstrip was heavily cratered, but a few planes remained. Early in September, the Navy's carriers started hitting the Palaus. Bomber and fighter planes from three fast carrier groups swept back and forth over the islands, finishing the work of the Army's heavy bombers. Naval cruisers and destroyers made bombardment runs against Peleliu and Angaur. Final pre-assault attacks began on the island. Pre-landing Naval gunfire objectives were the conventional ones: to soften up the enemy by knocking out his aircraft and his artillery and its emplacements.

This process, in addition to demolishing the above-ground installations, had also sheared a large part of the jungle growth from the north-western ridges, but the Japanese suffered negligible casualties.

9: American Strategy

Destiny brought us to the Palaus. Fate has stacked the deck. What are the cards that she, fate, will deal out to us? We, of the 710th Tank Battalion, are supporting the Army's 81st Infantry Division. The 81st in turn are the floating reserve and support forces for the First Marine Division. This unity made the Army and the Marines partners in our dealings with fate, we would not bluff. We had to play the hand out.

The First Marine Division's battle plans were finalized. The division's three Regimental Combat Teams would land abreast. The 1st Marine Regiment would put ashore one battalion in assault on each of the White Beaches, with the 3rd remaining battalion in reserve.

Their missions: drive inland through the barracks area, then wheel left and attach the nose of the ridge of the north western peninsula. It was understood that with having the high ground as their objective, the 1st Marines had drawn the toughest assignment. Although the contours of the high ground were still covered by vegetation, it was a foregone conclusion that the Japanese would have plenty of heavy weapons emplaced there.

The 5th Marines would land on Beaches Orange 1 and 2, the battalion on the left tying in with the 1st Marines, the other driving straight across to Peleliu's eastern shore. The support battalion would land at H plus one hour, move in between the other two battalions and attack across the lower end of the airfield, then turn northward, and after securing the airfield seize the flat north-eastern peninsula and the out-lying islands.

The 7th Marines, less one battalion that was kept afloat as division reserve, would land on Beach Orange 3, drive across the eastern shore on the flank of the 5th Marines, wheel right and mop up enemy contingents in its drive to the southern tip of the island.

With this battle plan, it would be possible to land on a wide front, having straight and clear approaches to the beaches, across not too bad a reef. The airfield and comparatively open ground to the south was suitable for tank operations, and it was anticipated that the drive across the island could be completed in short order. The disadvantage of driving across open flat terrain commanded by the high ground to the north was clearly if not fully realized. Although the contours and topography of this high ground were still hidden by jungle growth and vegetation, past experience made it a foregone conclusion that the Japanese would have plenty of heavy weapons dug in there. It was anticipated that the 7th Marines would complete its assignment the first day, and become available to regroup and support the 1st Marines, so that the striking power of the two combat teams could concentrate on the high ground in a short time. It was planned to support the 1st Marines with a maximum of air and naval gunfire, artillery and tanks, until the 7th Marines could complete its initial assignment.

General Rupertus displayed reluctance in the use of Army troops, and according to the original overall plan, there was what appeared to be an ample margin of safety: the 81st Infantry Division was not to be committed on Angaur until the situation on Peleliu was well in hand.

Aboard our LST we learned that the basic planning of Stalemate 11 called from the First Marine Division to land on Peleliu on September 15 (September 14—International Date line, west longitude date—my birthday); then, unless the Marines encountered more trouble than anticipated, the Army Wildcat Division (81st Infantry) would land on Angaur a few days after the critical assault phase on Peleliu had been successfully completed. Total troop strength of Stalemate 11 now amounted to about 50,000 men. The First Marine Division accounting for more than 28,000 and the reinforced 81st for about 21,000. A Regimental Combat Team of the 81st would also have the job of seizing Ulithi.

As our convoy neared the Palaus, we received the optimistic word that the pre-assault bombardment would knock out at least half of the Japs, so the operation would be short and simple. On board ships carrying the First Marine Division, and accompanying newspaper reporters and troop commanders, was a sealed letter from General Rupertus. Upon opening it was found to state that the fight would be a rough one, with casualties—but it would be over quickly. General Rupertus predicted that Peleliu would be captured in four days, perhaps less. Japan's Lieutenant General Sadae Inoue, with orders straight from Imperial General Headquarters to hold the Palau Islands at all costs, had other plans. General Rupertus did not have any inkling of the carnage his troops were to receive.

In combat, every man has fear—the greatest percentage of men control their fears and emotions and try to inspire their fellow buddies with their control of these emotions. Fear creates more fear.

The coward cannot and will not control his emotions.

I have to salute the foot soldier, the Infantryman, and honor and give all the respect due him. These men have to fight for every foot of land to be conquered. They, the Infantry, as the invaders of a fortified enemy stronghold, are exposed to well-dug-in and entrenched enemy forces. Normally these cleverly camouflaged strongpoints or positions are revealed only after the infantry come under fire; then—only then—are these positions exposed and made known. These ghoulish procedures are necessary, and the results are casualties and deaths. These are all branches of our military work for these gallant men, our Infantry. The Navy brings them to their destinations. Our Navy takes aerial and ground surveillance of the enemy's positions. The Navy's Air Force bombs these positions. The Navy lays in a pre-landing bombardment with their heavy naval guns and acts as support when needed and called upon with their weapons of war. Our Navy also acts as a delivery service, supplying our forces with everything that can be helpful and necessary in aiding the Infantry to obtain its objectives. Our Air Forces strafe, bomb, and drop a jellied gasoline mixture that is ignited. It's called napalm. If in direct contact with it you burn; if you do not burn you suffocate from the lack of oxygen which the napalm consumes while burning. Our tanks are brought directly to points of resistance for their firepower, various artillery guns up to six inches (155mm–155s) in diameter are brought into action, but still it's the ground troops—the Infantrymen—who have to slug it out, sometimes in hand-to-hand combat.

Our ground forces, particularly the Infantry: I salute you.

10: Japanese Defense Tactics

Remember the Bushido Code: honor, courage, loyalty; the ability to endure pain in silence; self-sacrifice, reverence for the Emperor and contempt for death? The Japanese moral code held that voluntary death was better than living in shame. Suicide was regarded as an honorable act. In training the Japanese recruits receive punishment, sometimes for trivial offenses, to make them respect authority and to harden and build up each soldier's endurance. When beaten, the recruit had to remain silent and appear indifferent to his pain—otherwise all others of his unit would undergo the same punishment. No recruits were spared, not even those from rich aristocratic families.

No living Japanese soldier was honored with any decoration or promotion for outstanding bravery in combat. Devotion and bravery were *required* by military code as a matter of course. If a hero was given a decoration or promotion, it was always after his death. Japanese soldiers were expected to die rather than accept and endure the humiliation of defeat. The Japanese fought with ferocity and frenzy, particularly when for the first time their homeland was threatened.

Very few prisoners of war among the defeated Japanese soldiers were taken in the whole course of the Pacific War. These were the troops, the enemy, that the American First Marine Division and the 81st Infantry Division would face as they invaded the Palau Islands.

On April 24, 1944, General Inoue's 14th Division reached the Palaus. Inoue's orders were brief and direct: secure the Palaus and Yap; these islands must be held to the very last.

Imperial Japanese General Headquarters issued new tactical defensive measures. Troops in the Palaus were instructed to be employed in new defensive tactics that were learned at Saipan. No more suicide attacks at the beaches in the attempt to annihilate the enemy at the waterline. They would knock out the American beachhead before it was consolidated, failing to accomplish this,

Inoue's defensive measures called for his forces to withdraw to carefully prepared and dug-in defensive positions. Defense of the beaches would be restricted to delaying actions. The main defensive activities would take place inland. Troops who were overrun at the beaches were to remain hidden, then to attack the Americans from the rear. The troops were told that merely dying for the Emperor while giving up the Palaus would not help their cause. Inoue planned and instructed his officers in the use of seven separate counter-attacks, which were to be set into operation by the firing of a distinctive flare at night or at the movement of a displayed flag. These defensive measures were a radical departure in and from conventional Japanese military thinking, and the 1st Marine Division was to pay a heavy price.

To carry out his missions, Inoue established his headquarters on the island of Koror, commanding about 35,000 troops in the Palaus and additional troops of 8,000–10,000 on the island of Yap. Inoue expected the main battle of the Palaus to take place on the large island of Babelthaup, and concentrated about 25,000 of his troops there. Peleliu, with its strategic airfield, was defended by some 10,500 men. Angaur had 1,400 troops. These defensive forces lacked air and naval support, as the American aircraft carrier strikes had destroyed practically all Palau-based aircraft, and the Japanese Naval Fleet had steamed westward.

But General Inoue's forces, inspired by Divine Inspiration, were capable and would put up a battle. Offshore and beach obstacles were emplaced. Mines were planted, both ashore and in the waters. Reinforced concrete gun emplacements and dug-in artillery positions that would cover landing areas with devastating fields of fire were laid out and employed. Inland, from the beaches, areas were heavily mined. Inoue's troops made good use of Pelelius' natural terrain and the island's features. Defensive positions composed of reinforced concrete and coral, expertly camouflaged, were situated so the defensive Japanese troops, while retreating, had lines of defense carefully prepared so that mortars and artillery could fire on previously registered target areas. The planned final resistance would take place in the caves and ridges of the high ground of the Umurbrogol Mountains, inland from the beaches.

11: The Allied Invasion—First Fire

On September 14, in the preliminary bombardment of the Palaus, Admiral Oldendorf, Commander, Western Gunfire Support Group (TG325), complained that he had run out of targets, profitable targets. His supporting gunfire had demolished most of the above ground installations.

At this time, we aboard our LST were invited and, yes, encouraged to view the power of our Armed Forces. This spectacle was very assuring, but I couldn't help recalling that as we shipped out of Pearl Harbor, we were denied the privilege of viewing the carnage the Japanese nation had inflicted on us.

Our LST was stationed about fifty yards behind a cruiser. This cruiser took part in the pre-landing bombardment. The firepower of our Navy was awesome. With each broadside (the firing of guns on one side of the ship), our LST would rock from the concussion.

The volleys from the firing of our battleships' 16 inch guns (explosive projectiles, 16 inches in circumference) gave us the illusion that the island would sink; nothing could possibly survive ashore.

Everything that was practical had been done. Naval gunfire and air strikes had presumably softened up the Japanese defenders. Minesweepers cleared the shipping lanes, Underwater Demolition Teams from our Navy had cleared the landing approaches and scouted the reef. Direct supporting fire with high explosives to knock out beach defenses then began. Smoke shells were exploded inland to screen the American invading forces. The Marines crowded into landing craft. Loaded landing craft circled a safe distance away from Japanese shore batteries while the first wave of our invaders formed up and got organized.

Under the smoke cover the first wave moved toward shore. Naval gunfire was moved inland away from the landing beaches and to the flanks or sides of the landing areas. Aircraft from our carriers strafed and dive-bombed directly in front of the landing craft.

As our forces neared the beached, the Japanese opened up with their shore batteries. High explosive projectiles began to fall among the landing craft, throwing geysers of water skyward.

As the covering smokescreen dissipated, we aboard ship saw the burning and wrecked assault vehicles. The Japanese refrained from revealing their defense positions by returning fire during our pre-landing assault fire. Our bombing and Naval gunfire had failed to knock out most of the Japanese weapons. General Inone's defensive measures had placed artillery deep in caves, protected by pillboxes.

The assault craft included LCMVs (landing craft, men and vehicles), amphibian tractors (LVTs), armored amphibian tractors, (LVT-A), amphibious trucks (DUKWs), and LVTs: every type of vessel was to be utilized. Tanks and crews were aboard LSDs, seagoing dry dock vessels, which carried LCTs (landing craft, tank). A tank would be pre-loaded aboard a LCT, then loaded under its own power into a flooded dry dock compartment. The dry dock compartment, after receiving its load of tanks aboard the LCTs, was then pumped dry for its trip to its destination. Once there, the compartment would be reflooded, the LCT would be afloat and proceed under its own power to the reef's edge and discharge its cargo—a tank waterproofed to get to the beach under its own power. The balance of the assault forces and their supplies were transported in PAs (personnel), AKAs (cargo) and Landing Ship Tanks (LSTs), the conventional assault transports. Two APHs (hospital transports), armed, and claiming no immunity in combat, would be on hand to care for the wounded. In addition, four regular hospital ships were also made available. The APAs were also prepared to care for the wounded until adequate hospital facilities were obtained ashore.

D-Day, September 15, began warm and clear. The ocean surface was calm, visibility unlimited: a so-called perfect day for an amphibious assault.

Original planning called for two days of pre-landing bombardment. This was revised upward to three days. This gunfire sheared a large part of the jungle growth from the north-western ridges of the high ground, the Umurbrogol mountain ridge. But General Inoue's network of fortifications had barely been touched.

The Marines landed on a mile-long front, three Regimental Combat Teams abreast alongside the airfield.

They saw the Umurbrogol, and it appeared to be small and innocent.

Aboard ship, as the screening smoke dissipated, we began to witness the horrors of war—the burning and wrecked assault vehicles. As the final pre-landing bombardment moved inland and to the flanks, the Japanese came out of their caves and strongholds. Inoue's defensive measures of concealment and fire discipline were paying off. The Americans were about to pay a heavy price for the coral real estate known as the Palaus. As our tracked assault vehicles crossed the Peleliu reef, they came under fire from the Japanese artillery and mortars. Some were hit, but most continued gamely in. At 0832 hours, two minutes behind schedule, the first wave touched down on the beach. On the left, Col. Puller's 1st Marines hit White Beaches 1 and 2; the 5th Marines in the center landed on Orange Beaches 1 and 2 on the right, Orange Beach 3 was the 7th Marines' assignment. As the amphibian tractors touched down, the Marines unloaded and ran on the beaches' hot sand, racing inland.

On the right, Orange Beach 3, obstacles and unexploded landmines forced the 7th Marines' Amtracs into a single file, making them easy targets.

On the left, White Beaches 1 and 2, Col. Puller's men came under heavy fire from a rocky point that became known as "Old Baldy". Only in the center, Orange Beaches 1 and 2—the airfield area—did the 5th Marines land intact. Soon the beaches were littered with the wrecked and burning hulks of assault vehicles—but still the landings continued. We had won a foothold, and an hour after the first wave reached shore, Sherman Tanks were landed. The Shermans received special attention from Japanese artillery and mortar positions. But now the Sherman Tanks could and would provide allied support to and for the Infantry.

General Inoue, overseeing the defenses of the entire Palau Island Group, was on another island. His subordinate on Peleliu, Colonel Kunio Nakagawa, carried out the new defensive tactics planned for Peleliu by Inoue. These tactics, a new and complete change in the Japanese military thinking, would have our troops catching hell and paying heavily.

On the naval cruiser *Portland*, a gunnery officer using binoculars watched as a heavy steel door opened on the side of a ridge. A Japanese artillery piece was then pushed out to the south of the cave, fired at the beaches, pushed back into the cave and the camouflaged steel doors were closed. The gun disappeared. The *Portland* laid in five salvos with its 8 inch guns. Between salvos the Japanese gun emerged from the cave untouched, firing and creating havoc with the Marines on the beach. The gunnery officer of the cruiser *Portland* said that we could put all the steel in Pittsburgh into that cave, and still we would be unable to knock out that piece.

Colonel Nakagawa, obeying General Inoue's directives, pulled the greater part of his infantry off the beaches to prepared defensive positions, and to counter-attack. On the morning of D-Day, September 15, our ships, the floating reserve, steamed north to the big island of Babelthaup. There we attempted to deceive the Japanese into thinking that Babelthaup was our next objective. By this time we were hoping that Inoue would not send Babelthaup troops as reinforcements to Peleliu. En route to Babelthaup, I used the tank's radio to listen to our Navy fighter planes as they strafed and bombed exposed enemy hot spots. Our Navy also had Observation Planes trying to locate targets for the bigger guns aboard our battleships. Listening to these pilots work in their quiet unexcitable manner was assuring for a young kid like me, who was about to participate in an armed shooting conflict—*war*.

I watched the spectacle of pre-landing bombardment, then the invading Marines assaulting a Japanese stronghold. The aircraft from our carriers were doing their damnedest to help our troops. A beautiful show, maximum effort, but Inoue's defense and defensive measures were taking an exacting toll of American lives.

The floating reserve returned from Babelthaup in the early evening, and our First Sergeant notified us that these Marines were in trouble. We were to land on Peleliu in the morning at eight o'clock. We were to get and have everything in combat readiness.

A funereal stillness overcame our compartment. The banter, horseplay and bull was noticeably missing. Everybody was obviously concerned with these new developments and wondered what the future had in store for them. A jerk in another platoon started sounding off about how he was going to kill Japs. It was quite apparent that he was shooting his mouth off to mask his fear. Numerous dirty looks did not quiet him down, and he was finally told to shut up. Fear! Everybody has fear.

We, kids going into manhood, were now faced with coping with our nation's enemy, Japan. Our only knowledge of the Japanese soldier that we now were about to encounter on the field of battle was meager; we were brainwashed with propaganda and biased Government documentaries. Hollywood's movies were a definite crock of shit. The combat veterans who instructed us during our training phases were believable, we hoped. But the question always persisted, were the situations and conditions altered, to inflate the egos of our instructors? In our quarters you sensed the fear, the fear of the unknown. The boys were expressing their fears, directly and indirectly. The men were coping and containing their fears.

This was understandable. We were kids, many pampered by loving parents, kids who never got knocked down or kicked by life; a gentle kick in the ass would have helped a good many of them. These kids were about to receive their baptism of fire, boys who were about to become men, under enemy fire, and combat veterans. The cowards—and there were many—would become known. Our country could not and would not overcome its enemies through acts of cowardice.

My platoon, especially my tank crew, appeared to be holding up well. One of the crew was missing, Harve; I did not attempt to locate him as I had to clear my own mind, and get my thoughts in order with these new and unexpected developments. I went topside and looked at the island of Peleliu. There in the dark of the night on the ocean's horizon was a black ass—the island of Peleliu. I watched and wondered. Flares discharged and ignited above the island illuminated areas of supposed enemy activity. The resounding retort of our infantryman's weapon, the 30 caliber M1, were heard. The very discernable sound of a sewing machine, the firing of a Japanese machine gun, was distinctly heard. The explosions of the projectiles from small knee mortars, which the Japanese soldiers were noted for and very adept with in its use, could also be heard aboard our ship.

I watched and wondered if, as we were forewarned, the buck-toothed Jap with the heavy horn-rimmed glasses was infiltrating our lines and bayoneting our troops in their foxholes. We were about to experience, at first hand, *war*. Knowing that at the crack of dawn tomorrow it would be harrowing and difficult, and believing that fate ruled my destiny, I went below and hit the sack.

WHAT'S TO BE SHALL BE...

12: Angaur Island and Bloody Gulch

Reprieve—September 16, 1944. After consulting with Regimental Commanders, General Rupertus did not request that we, the floating reserve, be committed at Peleliu. The Marines did not want green troops to receive their baptism of fire in this hell-hole called Peleliu. The First Marine Division would hold on and do the job. Stalemate II operations plan called for us to be reserve to the First Marine Division; if unneeded, our assignment was then to assault and conquer the Island of Angaur. Two Regimental Combat Teams of the 81st Army Infantry Division were given that chore. A regiment was to remain as reserve; later in the day this Regimental Combat Team would assault and seize the island of Ulithi.

Angaur is smaller than Peleliu. Shaped like a rough half-moon, it's slightly less than three miles long and one and a half miles wide. It is mainly flat with high ridges in its north-west corner, where the Japanese dug phosphates; the Salome Bowl. Much of Angaur's shoreline is guarded by steep cliffs. A few small coral reefs fringe its coast. Angaur has several fine landing beaches. This island, Angaur, was much more difficult for the Japanese to defend than Peleliu. From the Japanese records and data captured at Saipan we knew that the garrison consisted of Major Ushie Goto's 1st Battalion, 59th Infantry plus reinforcing units—approximately 1,400 Japanese; not a strong force. Major Goto had to disperse his forces thinly to man his prepared defenses covering the excellent landing beaches. Our landings received full preliminary landing treatment—naval gunfire, rocket barrages, strafing and bombing from naval aircraft. Additional support came from the 8th 155 MM Gun Battalion. They fired shells about six inches in diameter. These guns were positioned on southern Peleliu and registering (shelling) Angaur. The Angaur Attack Force consisted of two battleships, five cruisers and five destroyers. Every known or suspected target was hit.

On the morning of September 16, Admiral Blandy, Commander

of the Naval Attack Force, reported that as a result of his forces' activities, the opportunity for a successful landing on Angaur was at hand. General Rupertus on Peleliu did not object. The assault on Angaur was set for 0830 the next day, September 17. On September 17, at the crack of dawn, the landing beaches began to receive the full treatment. Salvo after salvo was laid on the landing beaches and on the Japanese defenses. The beach that we were to land on was not one of the carefully defended beaches, but a beach in an area on the north-eastern section of the island. This area was now designated as Red Beach. As there wasn't a coral reef to impede our landings, assaulting crafts were able to come ashore all the way into the beach, even the bulky LSTs. As our 81st assault waves came closer to shore, they began to receive light rifle fire and mortar rounds. Major Goto's troops had survived the bombardments and were ready to receive and hopefully to repel us, the invaders.

September 16 aboard our LST was spent tying our ends together and briefings. Our Company was ready to go to war. Physically we were in top-notch condition, equipped, trained and eager in some degree. After our prolonged cruise we were ready for dry firm land. Our mentality was highly questionable. On September 17 we received our final briefing. We were told not to get between the tanks. The tank drivers received specific instructions: put your tanks into first gear, gun the shit out of the engine, and fly off the LST's ramp and head for shore. Do not, and it was repeated, do *not* attempt to shift gears, slow down or stop while disembarking. Go inland, get away from the beach. The drivers started warming up their engines. Now in the LST's cargo compartment we had to contend with the heat and the roar of sixteen engines. The LST's hold began to fill with carbon monoxide and the ship's fans or ventilation system was not strong enough to remove the fumes. Our crew appeared to be holding up well, if maybe a little groggy. Harve was quaking with fear. Conditions being what they were it was understandable. One man threw up. Apparently, he did not enjoy the traditional steak and egg breakfast—real eggs, not dehydrated—prepared for us by the Navy. This is the standard breakfast called the "executioner's meal"— the last meal. It is furnished by the Navy for all assaulting forces on D-Day. Others seeing the vomit threw up too; one man passed out.

Our LST hit the beach and the tanks rear-ended each other as their forward motion continued, but the LST was stopped by the beachhead. The LST opened its bow doors and dropped the ramp. We were now getting some refreshing air, and the ship's ventilation system was becoming effective. The order to mount up (climb aboard the tanks) was heard. Surveying our exit ramp showed that it would be a water landing. Our LST was stuck a short distance from dry land. The Navy frogmen had reconnoitered the beaches. We hoped their findings were accurate. Bill, our driver, had our Cyclone airplane engine warmed up, he revved it up until it whined like a banshee. (The whining of a banshee, a female fairy in Ireland, usually signifies death in the family—was this an omen?)

Lt. Harol, communicating over the tank's intercom radio, told Bill and Harve to button up (close their hatches). He than secured his hatch and directed Bill to move out. We drove down the ramp and into the water. Our fate was now sealed. What did she, Fate, have in store for us?

The ocean enveloped our tank, its level coming up to our turret. Bill and the snorkels had done their job. We were on the beach, dry land. Harol's remaining four tanks of his first platoon also conquered the ocean. A land tank is not supposed to be a submarine, but ours were submerged beneath the ocean's depths. Lt. Harol of the First Platoon got his five tanks safely ashore, now it was Lt. Gavlik's Second Platoon's try at landing. But the lead tank of Lt. Gavlick's Second Platoon, the sixth tank to disembark, drowned; it was dead in the water and blocking the exit ramp. The Beach Party, trained and assigned for purposes such as this, pulled the tank out of the way with a tractor. The next tank of Gavlik's platoon, the seventh tank in line, also drowned dead in the water. Gavlik's remaining three tanks got off the LST in running and usable condition. Now it was time for the Third Platoon, and Lt. Caffin, to get his five tanks out. He did, Captain Richard in the sixteenth tank had no problems. C Company with these losses were short two tanks. The remaining operable tanks moved inland, away from the beach, which was zeroed in and registered with Japanese artillery.

Inland, we formed up, got organized and removed the snorkels. The snorkels had served their purpose; they did their job. Now we awaited orders. Kill Japs—kill more Japs, earn the $2 a day the Government was paying you. Go kill some Japs! An alliance was now being formed with the grim reaper. The ghastly and sordid detailing of war and its aftermath were now about to unfold.

On hitting the beach, we came upon the sight, a sight that shall remain in my memory for the rest of my life. Many more were to follow, but the first always remains with you, the first Americans killed.

We, the "good guys"—the Americans—did not have a binding contract with the grim reaper; the Japanese also got into the act, they had a contract with the reaper. My first killed-in-action sighting was an American youth, in his early twenties, laying on the hot sand, eyes open, starring skyward with his right hand pointing to the heavens, a gold wedding band on his ring finger.

Our Infantry, the Wildcats, came ashore on two separate beaches. Colonel Dark's 321 Regimental Combat Team (RCT) landed on Blue Beach, on the east coast, just below the center of the island. The 322nd RCT hit Red Beach on the north-eastern shore.

Encountering no organized beach defenses and only moderate small arms fire and mortar shelling, the Wildcats worked their way inland. The 81st Infantry, the Wildcats, were not long in discovering why Major Goto had concentrated his strongest beach defenses elsewhere. Driving inland, both Regiments found themselves entangled in a jungle rainforest. Mother nature had provided Major Goto with an impenetrable barrier. Japanese snipers hidden in its thick foliage were a genuine menace. Machine guns spewed death upon the invaders from camouflaged bunkers. The jungle and the Japanese got their first casualties after an hour of back-breaking work to gain a hundred yards of beachhead. The Wildcats then moved quickly off the beaches to higher ground and set up a perimeter of defensive positions. We landed with our tanks. Assault and supply craft started piling up on the beach. Bulldozers went to work on the jungle, clearing storage areas and cutting a road through the forested island.

While the 321st and 322nd RCTs were landing on the east coast, Colonel Watson's 323 RCT staged a mock attack on Angaur's west coast. The Wildcats piled into their landing craft, formed up into assault waves and headed for shore, under a Naval bombardment of the Angaur beach and shore. With this feint, we were hoping to confuse Major Goto, hoping that he would pull troops away from the active beaches. Major Goto could have possibly been elated, thinking that he had driven off the invaders with his defensive preparations, on these the excellent landing beaches on the western, southern and south-eastern shores.

We joined forces with our assigned RCT, the 322 Regiment of the 81st Infantry Division, the Wildcats, inland from Red Beach. Our mission and work began. We worked over the northern sector, using and giving fire support to the advancing Infantry. Things were proceeding smoothly and the Infantry was moving ahead.

An urgent, excited call came over our tank radio on the flank assigned to C Co. "Help, *H-E-L-P*, they are going to kill us!" We recognized Lt. Caffin's voice. We wondered what in the hell was going on in Caffin's sector. This information, and the situation involving Lt. Caffin, his tank or platoon was not given to us over the airwaves. We had our own work to consider and do. The 322nd RCT had relatively easy going, and by nightfall we had succeeded in occupying the northern half of our assigned sector.

Our tanks were placed just behind the defensive perimeter that was set up for the night by the Wildcats. Our orders were to settle in for the night—any bodily functions that had to be done, do them now. Any movement after dark would draw fire; we could be shot by friendly American fire as well as Japanese.

We received the information that Caffin was about seventy-five yards inland from the beach, behind the front line of the advancing Wildcats. His tank had stalled, and his driver had encountered problems restarting it. Caffin became panicky, he and his crew then abandoned the tank, and with Caffin in the lead ran back to the beach. Our discussion of this "incident" reminded us of our Jungle Training escapades with Caffin. One of our crew, noting the conditions involved, was in sympathy with Caffin. The sympathizer was told that officers were directed to hide their fears, set an example and lead their men. It was noted that in the dictionary, sympathy was found between shit and syphilis, all not worth the powder to blow them to hell. Be grateful that Caffin was not bossing our tank! The bastard would get us killed.

Caffin, the coward, would command our tank before this campaign was over, and their would be problems. We prepared our sleeping areas. Not knowing what to expect, I decided that my best bet would be to remain in the tank; its armor would be my foxhole. Laying underneath the 75 I found sleep impossible; this confinement was like a prison. Leaving the security of the tank's turret, I lay on the deck behind the turret above the tank's engine. This was much better, fresh air to breathe and open spaces. After getting as comfortable as could be expected, I heard it. Lt. Harol blew air and then emitted the strongest bit of profanity I have ever heard him utter—"Darn, darn, darn!" Lt. Harol, being an officer and a gentlemen, was also a sharpie. He brought along an air mattress to sleep on. Apparently he did not take into consideration the nasty Jap who shot holes into his mattress! Harol disposed of his mattress and slept on the hard ground like the rest of us cannon fodder.

All was quiet, peaceful, just the usual jungle noises. Rifle fire was heard; this brought flares which illuminated the area of the shooting. The quiet of the night in our sector did not alleviate the tension of this nerve-racking experience; green troops facing a fanatical enemy on a heavily fortified island stronghold. Developments were toward the quiet side, no Japanese banzai attacks or any massive organized threats. As is common among all green troops, every time a jungle bird cawed or a branch crackled there would be rifle fire and exploding hand grenades.

The Japs *did* infiltrate our positions, some working over our foxholes, others seeking positions to the rear of our lines so they could harass us as snipers. All in all it wasn't too bad of a night. Dawn brought a valley of gunfire; the troops were releasing pent-up emotions and tension brought about by the landing on the beachhead, and their first night on the island existing under combat conditions. They were firing all of their personal weapons. A jungle bird, cawing and flying above our tank, appeared to be chased by tracer rounds of the GIs firing. I laid flat as I could on the engine deck behind the tank's turret and took advantage of its security, believing that if I rose I would take one (get shot), so I sweated the shooting out until the GIs settled down and quit firing. The tank's engine deck, with its light armor plate, not only protected the engine but it also served as our trunk. Space inside was very limited, every nook and cranny had to, and was used to, serve a purpose. Our bedding, GI cans of water and usually a couple of cases of combat rations (food) were secured to the engine deck.

Having air supremacy, we found our 50 caliber machine guns a pain and unneeded. We would have loved to dump them, but lacking guts we were forced to carry and care for these excess armaments. The 50, in its canvas covering case, was also tied down out of the way on the engine deck. Personal belongings such as our musette bags and weapons were tucked away where space was available inside the turret. Our precious cargo, the spam and pineapple, were stored on the turret deck. There were known thieves in our Company who would have no qualms in confiscating our loot, so we had to conceal it in the tank's interior.

Returning to our Company Base there was a sight to behold; a dugout composed of fallen palm trees reinforced with sandbags on both sides and on the top. Offering beautiful protection, it would take a direct hit from a Naval gun to penetrate the enclosure our Company Truck Driver, Moose, had built. Moose had spent the day creating his masterpiece; he was the envy of the entire Company. Moose had his security. He could and now would get a good night's sleep.

Our tanks rejoined the Wildcats. Their objective—link up with the 321st RCT and consolidate the two beachheads. This link-up was originally scheduled as the first day's objective.

On the first day of the invasions, Major Goto was apparently unsure of the American intentions. Was the feint attack on his west coast the real thing? How many Americans were landed on the two beaches to the east? Goto played a cautious hand; he committed an infantry company to the beachheads. He withheld and maintained the bulk of his forces inland. Except for scouting patrols, checking on the invading Wildcats, Major Goto did nothing during the first day. Goto probably was influenced and concerned about the condition of his troops, who had survived the continuous air and naval bombardment.

This first day, the Wildcats did not have to contend with the Japs. They had enough problems with what mother nature provided Goto for his defensive measures: a rainforest of overgrown trees with thick roots, bushes and twisted vines; an impenetrable mass of jungle growth torn and matted by the pre-assault bombardment, and the heat: temperatures of 115°—that's 105° in the shade, if you could find the shade. Water, drinking water, became a problem. Water supplied to ground troops came from overworked amphibious tractors and landing craft, they were unable to ferry sufficient amounts of drinking water ashore. Some of the water ferried ashore was stored in improperly cleansed oil drums. GIs consuming this water vomited and soon became debilitated. The lack of salt tablets caused the heat prostration casualties to rise alarmingly. Emergency calls were made to all ships offshore requesting every available salt tablet.

Machines were placed into service which removed the salt from ocean water and a palatable drinking water was obtained. Within days, wells were drilled, and we finally had a sufficient supply of drinking water.

We now had our food—combat rations—our bedding, and fresh water. Now we only had to protect our asses and cope with the tropical heat.

The best and only way we had to accomplish this was to remove the Japanese presence from this island, Angaur.

We started; we made substantial advances during our first day in assault, and we survived our first night. We now thought that we were seasoned veterans, combat veterans, we were ready to cope with conditions and overwhelm and conquer the Jap. Our second day found us fighting our way to the western shore and the phosphate plant. En route we encountered a miracle: there was a live horse in an open area. Lt. Harol notified me that if I killed the horse, he would court-martial me. This horse had survived the pre-assault bombardment and all the invasion activities. He was entitled to live.

Our drive to reach our objective this second day was also unsuccessful; we did not reach the western shore.

Our second night was a nightmare. The Japs were out. The night began with the expected jungle noises. The birds were cawing and they also were settling down for the night. Then we heard the birds complaining and the flapping of their wings as they flew away. Now a quiet and stillness prevailed. Suddenly all hell broke loose; the Japs opened up with machine-gun and small arms fire. You could hear the

Japs activating their grenades by rapping them upon their protective metal helmets. The muffled explosions of these grenades resounded throughout the jungle. Flares illuminated our front, but the canny Jap knew how to prevent revealing his image while flares were illuminating the area. Upon hearing the small pop which activates the flare, he, the Jap, would freeze, thus making him very difficult to locate. After creating havoc with our outposts, and harassing the troops on the line, the Jap would withdraw. He had accomplished this night's objectives.

Then phase two would start. The jungle returned to its stillness. We returned to our sacks, hoping that that was it for the night so we would get much needed sleep and rest for our next day's "adventures" into the unknown. Then it began, the moaning and calling for help. Our American passwords for the night always contained the letter "R". The Japanese were unable to manage the pronunciation of this letter; in their speech, "sorry" would sound like "solly".

The gut-renching call and moaning continued… was it a wounded American or a Japanese ruse? After staying awake and hearing the moaning and groaning, even our GIs hoped that whoever he was, American or Japanese, would die or someone would kill him and put him out of his misery.

With the headcount at dawn, we were notified that C Company had suffered its first casualty; a man from the second platoon got killed.

If the Jap sustained any casualties, they were withdrawn along with Major Goto's troops. Goto's patrols accomplished its purposes. We green GIs spent a sleepless and very nervous night. Goto's patrols showed us, the American forces invading Goto's island, that Angaur defenses were stable and firmly organized.

Major Goto then began to shift his forces from southern Angaur to the Romauldo Hills in the north-west sector of the island, where he planned on making his final stand. His withdrawal was a rapid one. The Jap withdrew carrying only what he could on his back. His artillery, heavy equipment and supplies were left behind. During the night, Goto had successfully withdrawn his men and now ordered a final harassing counter-attack. We, with the 322nd RCT, endured several small attacks. The 321st RCT on Blue Beach to the south bore the brunt of Goto's attacking force. The Jap counter-attack only delayed us slightly. We pushed onto the phosphate diggings. The heavy jungle and rough terrain slowed our progress. Driving into Saipan Town on the western coast, south-west of the phosphate plant, we came upon the remains of the so-called Saipan Town; a thatched hut, probably the residence of a Jap officer, and a galvanized sheet metal shed, about eight feet high and about sixteen to eighteen feet long. Lt. Harol ordered me to fire a 75 MME (high explosive) round into this shed, which was about forty yards to our immediate front. I obeyed his order. I fired, and the high explosive projectile exploded about fifty yards to the rear of the shed. Lt. Harol inquired, "What's the matter with you, Luzinas? Can't you hit the side of a barn?" He was serious.

Stunned! Dumbfounded! I examined my gunnery; the target was immense; my sights, both bore and periscope, were aligned; the range was very short, so what happened? The solution came. I turned to Lt. Harol and asked him if he wanted the explosion in the storage shed. Then I proceeded and quieted him down. I fired, and the projectile exploded in the shed. The business end of a 75 MM shell, the projectile of HE, has a delayed action fuse; it explodes a fraction of a second after the projectile makes contact with the target. Rather than changing the timing fuse on the nose of the projectile, I ricocheted it into the shed. By aiming and firing short, the projectile bounced or skipped into the shed and exploded.

Pushing north to the diggings, we came upon a railroad bed with the steel tracks spaced for narrow gauge railroad cars, such as the ones used in the Hawaiian Islands. It was very noticeable that our Wildcats were working, and working very well, as a good many Japs were strewn around the area, all dead.

Our driver, Bill, entered the hut and collected a souvenir, a stuffed iguana, a good-sized lizard that resembles a prehistoric dinosaur, but not as large. Bill then mounted his souvenir atop the tank's turret. Apparently this iguana must have been the Jap's mascot, and they were annoyed. As we pushed north they started shooting at us.

It must be noted, as it was quite noticeable to me, that the Combat Wildcat, the footslogging GI working the line, respected and honored the Jap. He, the American cannon fodder, did not—I repeat, did not—desecrate the bodies of the dead Japanese. This profane violation of a body was accomplished by the rear echelon scavengers. This scavenging was a problem that had to be and would be dealt with. Our scrounger, Bill, reported that he did not have any luck in finding a prize souvenir: a Japanese officer's Samurai sword, or the thousand-stitch waistband worn by the Jap for luck. To obtain the waistband you had to ravage the body of a Jap whose luck ran out and no longer needed his good luck adornment.

Oh, yes, these souvenirs would bring our crew whiskey and or money, usually the rear echelon officer's monthly ration of whiskey. My guess was that the rear echelon boys wanted to display their souvenirs and brag about how they won the war.

Well, we were not lucky today. Maybe tomorrow we could make connections and get some booze.

Our drive to the Ramauldo Hills and Major Goto's line for his final defensive stand in the phosphate diggings was held up. We returned to our Company Base for much needed rest and reorganization. To cope with the tropical heat and the glaring sun we extended the tank's tarpaulin between four palm trees. We now had a degree of coolness and a slight breeze under the tarp. You guessed it, first one of the Company's officers came over, another soon followed and the next thing we noticed and realized all of the officers were approaching. They took over and we were back out in the sun.

The Company's Maintenance Sergeant, a five-striper Technical Sergeant whose job was to keep our vehicles running, came over to our tank and started chewing my ass out. I don't know if the jerk was trying to impress the officers or what. There was sand on the tank's suspension system (boogie wheels and framing which held up the tank's tracks). He directed me to clean up the tank. I looked him in the eye and said, "Sarge, do you want this tank cleaned up?" He said, "Yes." I told him that if he wanted this F— tank cleaned to pull the rag out of his ass and start cleaning. I told him that we were not playing games on the line. We were pulled back for a rest, and this crew was going to get some rest.

The officers heard this discussion and maintained their silence; they would not get involved. The jerk, the Sergeant, walked quietly away.

We then made our daily drive to the ammo dump. There we disposed of yesterday's spent shell casings and replenished our ammunition. This required the work of four of us: one to remove the 75s from the protective cardboard coverings, another to hand the uncovered 75 shell to the man atop the tank, and he in turn handed it to the leader, who stored them. As we fired an average of ninety shells a day, this replacement became a daily grind. Next we drove to the gasoline storage area or dump to gas up. This was a tedious but not as exhausting a job as the loading of the munitions. The gas was already stored in convenient jerry cans. One man on the ground would attach a pouring spout or nozzle to the can and hand it to the man on back, the engine deck, who then poured the gas into the tank's storage receptacles. Our tank never normally needed much gas because of the smallness of the island, and we never had to travel far to get to the action.

We were now prepared for any eventuality. Returning to our base, we enjoyed the hot food and the hot coffee our cooks had prepared for us. They served us delicious freshly baked sour-dough biscuits that were appropriately named hard tack; we called them dog biscuits. All in all our cooks were to be commended, and I shall commend them. Considering what they had to work with, they fed us well.

Yes sir: we were fed, our tank was loaded, we now looked forward to taking a breather and hoping to relax our nerves.

No such luck: the order came, "Mount up!" (Armored Forces originated from the Army's horse cavalry units. "Mount up" meant to climb up and enter your tank.) Division expected a banzai attack. The Japanese banzai attack was normally a drug and or alalia-induced stupor, with a suicidal frontal attack on our lines and outposts, following the Bushido Code. The end result of these fanatical assaults were the wasting of a good many Jap forces and creating tense temporary confusion with our GIs. For the Jap, it was his duty and desire to die gloriously for his Emperor.

We were to provide support and our firepower to the Infantry units working the expected point of the Jap attack. Our orders were to take the Company Radio Man, Riley, with us and dig in and wait for additional orders that we would receive over the radio.

We arrived at our designated outpost, dug a cavity and drove the tank over our trench. We turned on our radio and transmitter, and started li'l-Jo (auxiliary generator) to keep the tank's batteries charged. We settled in under the tank and prepared to spend an anxious and nervous night. It was a quiet night, a peaceful night. The Jap banzai never developed, but there were two casualties. While asleep, beneath the tank, Riley let go with a scream, flung his arms around and gave his head a resounding thump on the tank's belly. For a short period of time—tumult! We thought a Jap had got under the tank and was joining us. Riley then notified us that a land crab crawled over his chest and that his head ached. After a somber laugh we tried to get settled in again—one casualty.

In the morning, in good light, the Infantry unit occupying the line or outpost to our immediate front pulled out and went to the rear. Another combat memory that shall remain with me: a GI, probably in his early thirties but looking like an old man in his seventies, eyes glaring and dragging his M1 (rifle), walked in front of the tank. The GI appeared to be very nervous and ready to crack up. We, the tank crew, hoped that he would receive proper medical attention. Riley had a severe headache but this GI had big problems.

Division wanted an airstrip on the flat terrain of the south-western section of the island. Our next objective and attack was to focus on southern Angaur with orders to clear that area. Division mistakenly assumed that Goto had concentrated his main body of troops there. Our company of tanks, with infantry riding aboard each tank and with other infantry units on foot, encountered only moderate resistance. Goto had withdrawn his main body of men to the north-west high ground, where he was still holding excellent defensive real estate.

Angaur was finally declared secure at 10:30 A.M. on September 20.

The island was cut in two on a wide front, with the Jap isolated in three pockets, two in the 321st sector, and about 750 of Goto's forces in the larger pocket, the Lake Salome Bowl in the Ramauldo Hills, in the north-west sector. This large amphitheater-like depression, with a steam-driven bucket loader standing in the shallow Lake Salome, would be renamed Angaur Bowl by the Wildcats. Pits from the phosphate diggings and thickly jungled mountainous terrain surrounded the lake. Lake Salome and its surroundings resembled a large cup with the only entrance to the lake a narrow gauge railroad bed atop an embankment of diggings of dirt. This railroad cut provided the only passage through the vertical cliffs. The surrounding mountain walls were covered with vines and thick tropical vegetation.

Major Goto's defensive weapons, his artillery and anti-tank guns, were zeroed in on the railroad cut. His foot-soldiers were stationed in palm trees and atop the rugged rim of the mountains with its gullies and protective crevices. Major Goto had emplaced his infantry and weapons in prepared bunkers and positions to unleash a heavy crossfire on any invaders.

Reloading our tanks, we returned to base, chowed down, and hoped to get some rest for tomorrow's experience. We were organized, fed, had coffee and had a little breathing time. Our sleeping cubicle was underneath a large mass of coral stone. The ground protected our butts, while the overhanging coral protected us from the Jap mortars. We felt fairly secure. The main points of resistance were away from us, so we did not feel the need to establish and post guards. Now we hoped to get some sleep.

Sleep—that precious commodity required by all. Rest—a period of physical and nervous inactivity; a by-product, a very good by-product, of sleep.

On Friday, a monthly pay-day Friday, back at Polk during our training, I played poker all night. The next morning, a weekend Saturday, we were scheduled to see a War Department propaganda movie at the Post theater. When seated, I slept, so my Platoon Sergeant woke me and ordered me to stand and watch the movie. I slept standing up. In combat you have to stand guard and be alert. Your life, and the lives of your buddies—in our case or situation, the other four crew members, a total of five men—are depending on the courage and stability of the man on guard. If a coward is on guard you sleep lightly, if you sleep at all. A coward overcome by fear can be very costly... five lives.

Again sleep, a beautiful sleep was denied us. Last night it was the Jap banzai attack. Tonight, unbeknown to us, a Division Artillery Unit moved into our sector and set up firing positions directly behind our base. The Artillery opened up with their 155s, a softening-up bombardment of the north-west high ground, Major Goto's last stand, which was to receive the Wildcats' attention in the morning. The onset of artillery fire nearby was an event that startled us. Was it incoming Jap fire, or our own artillery at work? We had little if any sleep this night. Our orders from Division were clear: not a single Jap was to be left unattended. The Wildcats had completed mopping up southern Angaur. Our Artillery worked over the north-west high ground during the night. At 0600 hours, Division Artillery and mortars concentrated on the Lake Salome Bowl. At 0700, Navy planes strafed, fired rockets and dropped 500-pound bombs on Major Goto's defensive last stand positions. His men were prepared to fight and die.

We were ordered to go in. Lt. Harol's tank, the point, was in the lead, backed up by Sergeant Karle's tank with Harold "Ike" Grieb driving, Forest "Lightning" Kern as Assistant Driver, Dom as Loader and Gerl as Gunner. In turn, Karle's tank was backed up by our Platoon Sergeant's tank.

As we approached Saipan Town the stench of the rotting Jap bodies lingered in the air. We noted fresh kills, bodies now bloated by the tropical heat or infested with maggots or large blue flies in that place.

Our frontal assault, through the railroad out in "Bloody Gulch" began. The Wildcats fought their way up the narrow passageway. The Jap laid down heavy fire, and the Wildcats held up their drive. American Artillery and mortars were called in and they covered the areas of resistance with cover fire. The Wildcats resumed their advance behind our tanks. But as Lt. Harol's tank approached the railroad cut leading into the Bowl we discovered our way was blocked by an SPM 8, a lightly armored, self-propelled tracked vehicle with cannon used by the Infantry for reconnaissance. The burning wreck had got hit by Japanese Artillery as soon as it penetrated and cleared the railroad cut.

The Wildcats' drive into Lake Salome Bowl stopped. Rear echelon ordered us to "blow up" the wreck with our tank fire. I guess the rear echelon personnel saw too many Hollywood war movies. I fired at the vital spots of the M8 with high explosive (HE) and Armor Piercing (AP) shells. After about forty-five rounds of 75 MM fire we now had a wrecked M8 with forty-five additional holes in it. The wreck still blocked the cut, but our gunfire extinguished the fire. We then received new orders over our radio: push the M8 out of the way with our tank. Rear echelon continued cluttering up the airwaves with suggestions and advice. Lt. Harol mentioned that our medics were evacuating our wounded with stretcher bearers and there was additional Infantry up in front of us.

The "brain" in the rear then ordered the Infantry to "blow up" the wreck with satchel charges (thirty pounds of dynamite encased in a canvas satchel). As the Infantry proceeded with this "task", the Japs opened up with machine-gun fire. The Infantry dove under our tank leaving a satchel charge behind. This charge started burning and the tank's running engine sucked in the burning cordite fumes. What's next? We assumed that we were afire, we had no way of knowing what the situation behind us was as we could not see, and Karle's tank was not equipped with a radio transmitter. They would only receive, so we were not notified of occurrences behind us. After a few intense, very intense, moments we simmered down and regained our wits. The tank's engine while running circulated the air and cleared the tank's interior of the cordite fumes. The airwaves again were all cluttered up. Lt. Harol told the rear that the fire was out, our Medics and Infantry were working the area in front of the tank. Harol then suggested to the "brain" that we could pull the wreck out with our tank. The rear said that is what they wanted to hear and ordered us to pull the wreck.

A Japanese rifle was pointing out of the north of a cave. I figured that Harve might want to shoot his machine gun, so I told him to shoot up that Jap rifle. Our training was to fire the 30 caliber machine gun in short bursts of three or four rounds, this allowed the gun barrel to cool down a bit. Harve fired and froze, he fired a full belt— 250 rounds—without letting up. I chewed his ass out, I told him that we did not know what we would meet up with and that I might need his gun.

Our Battalion Commander (Lt. Colonel, 710th Tank Battalion) with a 45 caliber handgun on his hip, and our Company Commander (Captain, C Co.) carrying a 30 caliber carbine, walked down Bloody Gulch (the narrow passageway, so named by the Wildcats) and hooked our towing cable onto the wreck. Backing out of Bloody

Gulch, we pulled the wreck out and the entrance to Angaur Bowl was now open.

Lt. Harol told us that Intelligence said that the Jap gun could not hurt us. I told Harol that the crew of the wrecked M8 was probably told the same thing, and if the Army had any real intelligence we would not be here. Harol looked at me but ignored my statement.

We followed the railroad bed in Bloody Gulch to the cut leading to Lake Salome and the Angaur Bowl. Entering the Bowl on a narrow dirt ramp that was the railroad bed, our tank was hit. Chips of paint were flying around inside the turret; we were hit.

Maybe Army Intelligence has some intelligence, as the Japanese Artillery projectile did not penetrate our turret's armor. We drove out to the end of the ramp with Karle and the rest of the Company's tanks behind us. I do not know how many of the Company tanks entered the bowl, but Karle and our Platoon Sergeant's tanks were there, behind us. The ramp was short and our training required us to keep distance between tanks. The Jap Artillery had a field day. They peppered our tank and went to work on our track suspension system and track. The gun played hell with the Infantry; nothing could move until this gun was located and knocked out.

A Jap ran from one position to another in front of our tank. No fire order. I decided not to wait for fire orders, and to shoot at targets of opportunity as they presented themselves.

While staring through my periscope I spotted the Jap gun to our left front at the base of the mountain. The Jap fired, probably at us; a great cloud of yellow, brown and gray smoke emerged from the mountain. I immediately traversed our turret and laid 30 caliber machine-gun fire into the cave and stabilized the activity within the cave. Lt. Harol inquired, "Ed, what are you doing?" I told him that I'd located the Jap gun. Harol asked if I was sure of its location. He then ordered me to knock it out. I worked the area over with 30 caliber machine-gun fire and about eight rounds of 75 MM of HE. Our tanks and the Wildcats were no longer under enemy fire. The Jap gun was knocked out.

The Infantry now resumed its attack and attempted to mop up and clean out Angaur Bowl. This was slow and hard work and not very beneficial. To avoid being cut off by a counter-attack in our exposed positions during the night, our forces pulled out. Our day ended in frustration and no advances.

This day, a day that shall remain in our memory banks, was one that all Tankers dread.

We drove forward out on this narrow dirt embankment okay. But... how were we going to be able to return to our base? To back a tank under enemy fire the Tank Commander has to face the back of the tank, peep into his periscope and attempt to back his tank successfully. To do this he tells his driver to brake or stop the movement of a track that the tank rides on. The other track moves, and that is how the driver steers or changes the direction of the tank. Peeping through a periscope and moving a tank forward is a problem; backing is a nightmare. The Tank Commander's directions to his driver are reversed, his right hand is the driver's left hand. If he wishes to go to the right his orders to his driver are brake or just a plain left, this stops the movement of the left track and the moving right track shifts the tank to the right. Remember, the tank is progressing backwards. Backing a tank is quite difficult on the wide open spaces. Going forward, to change direction the driver has vision and he takes the track that leads in the direction that he wishes to pursue. To go right he brakes right; to go left, he brakes left.

We were sitting ducks on a raised dirt embankment on which the Jap had placed his railroad bed and track.

Now, how do we back up and get the hell out of this hell-hole?

We started. The third tank in line, the Platoon Sergeant's, backed out. He ran off the embankment, slipped down the slope taking a lot of the railroad bed with him, and ended with his tank's belly or bottom looking skyward, upside down. His crew tossed their smoke grenades so that the Infantry gave them covering fire. The crew of five evacuated the tank safely with no casualties.

Now it was time for our back-up tank, Sergeant Karle's—the second in line—to take a crack at backing up. Karle failed too. His tank slid off the ramp on the opposite side of the embankment, directly across from where the other tank slid off. Karle's tank also took a lot of the dirt ramp with him on his slide down the slope. We now had lost two tanks and Don, the loader and radio man, took a Jap hit. He got shot in the arm while evacuating.

Now it was the turn of the point tank, Lt. Harol's, to successfully try to get our tank out safely. We had problems, big problems, to surmount. The two previous tanks, in sliding off the ramp—one to the right, the other to the left—took a hell of a lot of the ramp with them. We had very little roadway, if you could call it that, left. If Harol attempted to back the tank out we would also slide down the embankment.

The Japs, after two such experiences, would now zero in on our tank if it became disabled. They would pepper the area even under the cover of smoke with rifle and machine-gun fire, and probably with their small but highly effective knee mortars too. Without our tank, our mobile foxhole, we were very vulnerable; we would most likely have part or all of our crew killed. Lt. Harol apparently did not place much credence in the ability of Sergeant Alvin, Commander of the fourth tank in line, to help us out of our predicament. The odds were against having Lt. Harol successfully back us out. Our Wildcats were of no help, even if they wanted to be, and I'm sure they would have helped; but they did not have the required knowledge to back us out with the use of the tank's telephone in the rear of the tank. You must also remember, and it has to be noted, that our tank was under enemy—Jap—fire. So, as I stated before, we had our problems; it was now our time to pray to the Lord again.

Our prayers were answered.

Oliver, our radio man and loader, volunteered to leave the security of the tank through the escape hatch located in the deck of the tank behind our assistant driver, Harve, and guide our driver, Bill—hopefully to solid land and safety. Bill and Harve unlatched and dropped the escape hatch cover, I traversed the tank's turret so the provided opening of the turret was above the escape hatch. Ollie dropped from the turret through the hatch and onto the ramp; he then crawled under the tank to its rear where the tank telephone was located. While directing Bill in the backing procedure—left-straight, right-straight—he came under a sniper's rifle fire. Using my 30 caliber machine gun with its tracer bullets, Ollie directed me toward, and I located, the area of the sniper. The sniper was in a tall palm tree to the left rear of the tank. I worked over both sides and the middle of the palm tree's trunk, up and down, with machine-gun fire. Ollie was no longer bothered by that sniper. But this encounter created some apprehension to our personnel in the tanks to our rear and the guys back at our base.

With the rear echelon bugging us with their constant questions over the airwaves of our radio, Harol told the rear that Ollie "got shot at". Harol did not realize in his radio transmission that he released his transmitter button on the very key word. His transmission over the airwaves was, "Ollie got shot."

Our Good Lord had showed us the path to take and guided us safely through this ordeal.

Returning to base to lick our wounds, we, found base relocated to the beach. Division expected Jap reinforcements from Babelthaup and hoped to repulse them at the water's edge, the beach. Our Company had dug a cavity on the beach, and we placed our tank over this cavity. Settling in for the night we hoped to unwind and get some needed rest. No luck: American troops that were to occupy the island had landed and were stationed directly behind our tanks. It was quiet, peaceful and serene, we were enjoying our breather. Then a land crab scampered across some corrugated sheet metal, and the crab's hard shell and claws striking the metal emitted resounding clicks. Our newly landed troops got shook! They opened up with rifle fire aimed at the sound, which was coming from the beach area. Ships of our Navy, expecting a Jap invasion, were stationed off the beach, and they came under the fire of the occupation troops. The Navy, believing that they were under enemy fire, started shooting back... Interesting, but very disturbing; we were stuck in the middle, the green occupation troops firing at night noises in the direction of our Naval units, and our ships returning their fire. After a bit, apparently everybody was ordered to cease firing and peace prevailed. We finally got some rest.

Sunrise found us examining our tank. We took a shell-shocking: the suspension framework that held up our track was demolished! The track's connectors that joined the track's steel blocks were blown off in two places, and the remaining connector on the inside of the track was the only thing holding the split track together and preventing us from losing our track and mobility.

As I stated before, the Good Lord was looking out after us. While examining our tank, Harve, our assistant driver, begged to get out of our crew. Reflecting back on incidents and the machine-gun bit in the gulch, I told Harve I would talk to Harol about removing him from the crew. Ollie was present during this discussion; I told Ollie that he had done more that his share and he should drop out too. It wouldn't do to stretch his luck, he had done a good, a damn good job; the Company had the crews—twenty-five men from the tanks that were inoperative. Let the "wheels" replace him and Harve, and he, Ollie, should take a rest. Ollie was reluctant, but after discussion and persuasion he agreed. He wished the crew luck and told us to call upon him if needed.

I informed Harol of the crew's situation, he stated that he would take care of our replacements.

Forest "Lightning" Kern, my buddy and Assistant Driver of the back-up tank (Sergeant Karle's, which overturned in the Angaur Bowl), told me that he was volunteering to come into our tank as Assistant Gunner. I told Lightning the hell with that crap. That he, Lightning, had done his job, and it was a damn good job. I added, "Don't stick your neck out, let the Old Man [Company Commander] get Harol his replacements."

Lightning looked me in the eye and said, "Ed, you're going, and I'm going with you."

That is the finest honor a man can receive—a buddy who is willing to put his life on the line to serve with his comrade under enemy fire. I have and shall ever cherish and carry that memory to my grave.

Karle's driver, Harold "Ike" Grieb, got wind of what Lightning was up to, and Ike joined up too.

Lt. Harol now had a tank crew. We could now sleep without having one eye and ear open. We drove the tank to Battalion Maintenance for the necessary repair work, they took over and we had a respite. Some excitement was developing at base. A makeshift raft was sighted off our beach; this raft was moving but we could not make out what was propelling it. An alarm was sounded and Lt. Gavlik, the Platoon Leader, Second Platoon, came charging to the beach. He resembled a general, a "take charge" guy. At the water's edge he came to a dead stop and ordered someone to swim out to the raft.

This order was wisely ignored. He then wanted a tank to shoot up the raft. Wiser heads prevailed; the Old Man told Gavlik that Division would be notified and the Navy would take care of the raft. I asked a Buck Sergeant of Gavlik's Platoon, the Second, what in the hell was going on with Gavlik—did he crack up?

The Sergeant replied that Gavlik was drunk on whiskey rations that the officers received monthly. He said Gavlik had a continual load on, and his Platoon Sergeant was covering for him. This reminded me that his tank had drowned while disembarking the LST. This yo-yo of an officer also wanted a souvenir of his exploits as an Army Combat officer. He finagled Espo, a kid gunner in my platoon, to attempt to disarm a fragmentary (pineapple) hand grenade. We were under strict orders not to fool with grenades.

When unscrewing the top of a grenade you encounter a thin copper cylinder containing black powder. This is a timing device, and after five seconds of activating the cylinder the black powder burns under compression, and this burning in turn sets off the cordite in the main body of the "pineapple", causing it to explode and send out flying hot missiles (fragments). Any hand grenade is extremely sensitive, not to be tampered with. Espo unscrewed the top of the grenade, tried removing the copper cylinder, and failed. The timing device exploded and Espo was peppered with copper fragments. The hospital cut him from his chest cavity down to his penis and across his belly, removing copper fragments. Espo lived. The navy took care of the raft and Gavlik carried on with his drunken stupidity.

Our tank was patched up, we reclaimed it and drove to the usual dump to reload and gas up. Combat Infantry officers, no longer vain but now combat-wise, wanted our Thompson sub-machine guns. They realized they wanted and needed the firepower of the 45 caliber Thompson; they also knew that a hand-gun or carbine was a sign to a Jap sniper that they were officers, the leaders, and the Jap snipers picked them off. A swap of weapons was arranged; the officers got our tommy-guns and we took their handguns, 45 caliber automatics.

We than went to the salvage grounds where the accumulation of battleground debris was stored, here we obtained M1 Garand-30 caliber infantry weapons. We were now covered for the loss of our tommy-guns.

While at this dump we procured some Signal Corps wire and dry cell radio batteries.

Give young men, in our case GIs, time that is untethered by military manure, and the usual result is some degree of mischief. This mischief is time-consuming, relaxing and very beneficial, especially to combat troops. It gives them something to bullshit about and helps relieve their anxieties. We were no different, and opportunity struck. We had electricity (dry cell batteries) and conductors (Signal Corps wire) and the impish desire of all youth. Lightning and I were not to be denied, we decided that Ike was to be our pawn. Ike had built a stand in which he placed his steel helmet so it would be elevated and convenient for his purposes. We decided to electrify the helmet—his washbasin.

We bared the insulation from both conductors (wire) and placed it under Ike's helmet. We attached the positive wire directly to the position terminal of the dry cell. Our negative wire was bared and buried in the ground. Our disconnect or switch was a bayonet. The wire from the negative or minus side of our electrical source (dry cell batteries) was then wired to our bayonet. By jabbing the bayonet into the ground we had our continuity, our electrical circuit was complete. You may think and say this was cruel and inhuman—it was creative genius! The dry cell batteries when activated would emit and allow amperage and voltage, so when placing your hand in the water you would receive a tingling sensation such as when you hand or leg falls asleep. We now had Ike's washbasin booby-trapped, but we would have to wait until morning to see our end result.

Command—our officers—also had their form of entertainment. A Jeep throwing gravel and sand swept into our compound. Our Battalion Commander emerged from the Jeep, legs astride, and barked, "Where is that son of a bitch Caffin? Get his ass out here!"

A very nervous and pale-faced Lieutenant appeared. The enlisted men of our Company were streetwise, and army-hardened explicit language was common. Our Battalion CO, an educator in civilian life, proceeded to educate us enlistees and officers alike. He started by pointing his finger at Caffin and ordered him, "Stand at attention, you bastard!"

He then notified Caffin that the machine guns he left behind when he abandoned his tank were being used by the Japs in Angaur Bowl, and our people are being hurt. Our education began, the CO climbed Caffin's frame up, down and sideways. Beautiful, beautiful… The CO put salt on the open wounds from his chewing by telling Caffin that he was a second looey now, and as long as he was under his command that was all he would ever be.

I wish I could end the chapter of the Second Lieutenant Caffin, Platoon Leader, Third Platoon, with the notification that Caffin remained a second looey—but our crew was to encounter and endure more problems with Caffin on Peleliu…

The entertaining and educating display of the CO's temper helped pass the time of day away. Now we were faced with another night on Angaur.

We got the password for the night and we were ordered to use hand grenades only; no rifle fire if the situation arose. As could be expected, a Jap paraded like King Tut at the water's edge on the beach in front of the line-up of the remaining tanks of C Co. The Jap threw a grenade at us, but fortunately he missed and the grenade exploded to the left of our tank, destroying a water can and some of our personal belongings. If that Jap had been accurate with his pitch, throwing it under the tank, he would have wiped out the whole crew—five men.

The remainder of the night was quiet, the occupation forces simmered down and our Naval forces did not shoot inland. We got some sleep. At dawn the body of the Jap could be seen at the water's edge at the end of the tank line.

Now we had the time and opportunity to devote to our washbasin escapade. Ike filled his helmet with water, and Lightning turned on the switch by jabbing the bayonet in the ground. The electrical circuit was complete. Ike placed his hands in the water to wet them prior to soaping. His hands received a tingle form the electrical impulse. Amazed, he withdrew his hands and stared at the sky. Lightning pulled the bayonet out of the ground, disconnecting the circuit. Ike decided to give it another try; he immersed his hands, no tingle… He reached for his soap; Lightning jabbed the bayonet back into the ground and the circuit was energized. Ike rinsed the soap from his hands and in so doing received the tingle again. He stepped back, scratched his head, stared skyward, and then scratched his fanny. But then our whistle-happy First Sergeant started blowing his police whistle to get our attention.

"Pack up, we are moving out, we are going to Peleliu!"

13: Peleliu and Death Valley

We'd outplayed Fate on Angaur, and I wonder what she had in store for us now at Peleliu...

The Marines needed help on Peleliu. We, C Co., 710th Tank Battalion, were reassigned to the 321st RCT of the Wildcat Division. The 321st, being the freshest unit, was being pulled out of Angaur. The 323 RCT was seizing the Ulithi Atoll 260 miles north-east of the Palaus.

The Ulithi group of about thirty coral reefed islands formed a large lagoon; a perfect natural anchorage for our large Naval vessels. Its land provided bases for extensive Naval installations as well as recreational areas. The 323 RCT, under Naval support and escort, landed on the Ulithi Atoll; to their delight they discovered that the Japs had pulled out. Friendly natives informed them that the Japanese had departed sometime before. Only a few graves remained.

Our Seabees got busy and worked on the lagoon for the Navy's Staging Area. An airbase was built, the ships of our Navy began arriving to support Admiral Halsey's Carrier Forces, which were headed for the Philippines to aid in that campaign which was forthcoming. Rest and Recreation Areas and Centers were developed. A hospital, baseball diamond, and both officers' and enlisted men's clubs appeared. White sandy beaches were available for bathing. Ulithi was the treasure of the Palaus, far more valuable in our push to Japan then either Angaur or Peleliu.

The 322 RCT remained on Angaur to mop up the remnants of Major Goto's forces. The 323 RCT was to assist after securing Ulithi and a number of outlying islands in the Western Carolines.

On October 23, after intense resistance by the Jap in the Lake Salome (Angaur) Bowl, Major Goto was killed and only Jap stragglers remained.

The seizure of Angaur by the 81st Infantry Division and its support units was at the cost of 264 Americans killed and 1,355 wounded. The Japanese nation lost 1,300 of its finest men on Angaur, all killed. An exceedingly large number—forty-five—of the Japs surrendered and were taken prisoners of war.

Our Company with its tanks and complementary units loaded on an LST for its trip to Peleliu. While steaming north ten miles to Peleliu, we heard the familiar thin, high-pitched whistling of the Naval piping. All hands; chow down. Being guests of our US Naval Transport, I told our tank crew to go and get some hot chow. We went to the ship's galley, and got into the serving line with the ship's complement of sailors. We got our trays and silverware and approached our first course—a large container of steaming white rice. With great expectations I extended my tray, hoping to receive a man-sized serving. The sailor rationing out the rice destroyed my illusion of a good meal. He said, "Sorry, Mate, we are not feeding Army, we did not prepare enough food!"

Rejected, we went to our tanks and obtained our lunch, cold combat rations—canned beans with franks. While "dining", we discussed the typical Army foul-up. Our complement of company officers was being served steaks in the Officers' Country (ship's bridge), while we, the cannon fodder, were consuming cold beans because our officers did not request our Navy to feed the Army personnel. We hoped they, our officers, got the GIs (excessive bowel movements) and/or indigestion.

Departing from our LST on Peleliu was unlike Angaur. The transport beached on dry land. We took our leave from the LST as tankers, not submariners. The natives (US Marines) accepted us in a friendly manner; they did not shoot at us.

Our Company Base was established just off the East Road and the beach, and near the southern section of the high ground, the Umurbrogol Mountains. To the south of our base was a curve in the road. This bend was named Dead Man's Curve, as a Jap sniper had zeroed in on this bend and was inflicting a good number of casualties on troops using the clearing. Patrols were unable to locate and weed out the Jap. So road signs were posted: DON'T STOP—SPEED UP–SNIPER AREA.

The "wheels", Command, now wanted us to earn our keep. We were ordered into the high ground, the Umurbrogol. The

Umurbrogol is mother nature's creation of hell on earth; a mountainous mass, the solidification of molten lava; a maze of gulches, crags, ridges and rubble and decayed coral; ravines which appeared to be steep-sided on aerial photographs were actually sheer cliffs, some fifty to a hundred feet high. This area of hell was renamed the "Five Brothers" (highest peaks) and the "Five sisters" (valleys) for obvious reasons. There were dozens of caves and pillboxes, each supporting the other with fields of fire from riflemen with machine guns, mortars, rockets and artillery pieces. General Inoue's defensive directive instructed his forces to run his weapons to the mouth of the cave, fire, then run the piece back into the cave before the Americans could react. The Imperial Japanese Naval Forces jointly occupying Peleliu had imported miners from the homeland to improve and enlarge mother nature's creations, the caves...

The generally accepted geological explanation is that Peleliu was once part of the ocean floor, thickly encased in coral growth which had been forced above the ocean's surface by volcanic action, the pressure buckling and cracking to form the maze of ridges and defiles; it also accounts for the steepness of the cliffs. A thin layer of topsoil above this bedrock sustained scrub jungle that was dense enough to screen. The volcanic pressures that created these weird surface conditions also developed underground faults in the coral limestone. Many of these faults were enlarged by erosion into natural caves. The Jap exploited these natural features and improved upon them.

Colonel Nakagawa's Command Post, located in a cave, had most of the comforts and conveniences of permanent quarters. He enjoyed a well-equipped galley, electric lighting, a communications center, wooden floors and built-in sleeping bunks.

Before the war, the Japanese had mined the island for phosphates. The miners and their techniques were used to improve and enlarge these underground coral complexes that honeycomb Peleliu, and to dig vast new caves, more than five hundred. One cave was well stocked with food and ammunition. Firewalls and bays were carved, sometimes by hand. Troops now could take refuge from American weaponry at the cavern entrances. Multiple entrances and connecting tunnels were dug by the miners. The deck was stacked in favor of the Japanese Empire. Peleliu had been mandated to Japan back in World War I.

Mother nature provided the Japs with a mountainous ridge approximately 2,000 yards long and 1,000 yards deep at its greatest depth; the Umurbrogol. Japanese miners with their resources improved mother nature's assets. General Inoue, using all these advantages and utilizing his military skills to serve his Emperor, chopped and chewed up our Marines. Savage fighting, heat, tropical rains and the Umurbrogol had taken their toll. The first week of fighting our Marines had suffered and endured nearly 4000 casualties of its combatant troops. On September 21, the III Corps Commander, General Geiger, told General Rupertus that his first Marine Division was "finished" and they should be relieved. We, the Army, the floating reserve, were being pulled out of Angaur to be the relief for our Marines.

The Army's job—our job—was to dig out, blast, and bury-kill the Japs and mop up the hell-hole called The Umurbrogol.

With prayer, sufficient toilet paper and a lump in our throats, we proceeded with our assignment.

We pushed to the Point. The Point, located at the southernmost edge of the Umurbrogol Mountain Range, was nature's gift to Colonel Nakagawa. Rising thirty feet above sea level, it was solid, jagged coral overlooking the airfield to the south, and to the north, the Umurbrogol with its mountains and valleys. Most notable, and to the left of the mouth or entrance to Death Valley, stood a huge gigantic boulder, Old Baldy. Old Baldy rose about fifty feet above ground level and it overlooked the airfield to the south. To its north lay the narrow valley with its coral mountains named the Five Brothers to the left and the China Wall to the right. This coral mass of nooks, crevices and caves, with its height looking down on the airstrip and the valley named "Death", provided Nakagawa with an excellent defensive position. He made good use of it for his Emperor.

Directly underneath Old Baldy, our Marines had built and provided us with a sandbag gun replacement, an outpost that enabled them and us to survey Death Valley and the airstrip.

While receiving instructions, we discussed and were advised by

Marines stationed there of the conditions and the situation that was facing us, the Army. A stench pervaded our surroundings; the stinking smell of rotting human flesh. We were told that the Jap was disposing his dead from the caves near the mouth of Death Valley, and it would be foolhardy for our forces to try to remove these corpses because we would be under the Japs' fire. The Marine directed us to look at the steep coral mountains with its caves and their firing slits. He then inquired if we had the foreboding feeling that we were being watched? He told us that we were under surveillance and not to expose ourselves. We were told of another nuisance, one greater than the Jap infiltrator. There were our Americans, the souvenir hunters; these jerks were being shot and Good Marines were being exposed to the Japs' wrath while trying to rescue the jerks. Of course the language used by the Marine was more aptly descriptive than "stupid jerk". The method used by the Marines to resolve the souvenir hunter problem was to round up the jerks and place them under an armed guard, who was under orders to shoot any resisters. These jerks were then put to work carrying water and ammo up to the front. The jerks complained that they would be AWOL (absent without leave). The jerks were told, tough shit—keep working! One bold jerk tried walking away from this detail. A 30 caliber round hitting the dirt in front of him brought him back in a hurry.

While conferring with the Marine, a man who was eavesdropping notified us that he was a correspondent for a stateside news service. I guess that this was supposed to impress us. He inquired of the Marine whether he had some souvenirs that he wished to barter. The Marine looked him in the eye and told the newsman, "I shall quote the *Marine Manual*: 'the only souvenir I want from this hell-hole is my ass'." Patting his fanny, he stated that it was still there and we were being pulled out.

I tried to swap our newly found handguns for some whiskey; no luck.

We began our daily forays into Death Valley. Most of these ventures were for the purpose of harassing the Jap, but a few were notable and worthy of mention.

Our Marines were withdrawn for much needed rest and

recuperation. It was now our turn to face and overcome General Inoue's challenges.

We went at it.

We were stationed and occupied the sandbag gun emplacement under Old Baldy.

The Wildcats, with our tanks in support, started blowing caves with satchel charges at the mouth of the Valley of Death.

The Valley of Death was a pocket in the coral mass about 250 yards long and about 75 yards wide at its widest point. It was enclosed by the China Wall to the south, or to the right of its mouth or entranceway, and to the left (or north) by another coral ridge. Both ridges rose forty to sixty feet above ground level, their composition was coral and they were full of caves and fissures.

To the right as you enter the Valley is a large cave, part of the China Wall. Inside the entrance to this cave we found another wall about eight feet from the mouth; this mass of coral was blocking the way. To enter this cave, you had to make a right turn, then left, to get behind the blocking wall and into the cave proper. This blocking wall stopped and prevented direct artillery or flame-thrower attacks. The miners from the Japanese homeland knew their work and they did it well.

Our work was cut out for us.

While the Wildcats were attempting to blow the caves with 30 pound satchel charges at the China Wall on the right, smoke and dust from the explosions was rising from the back or far side of the steep coral ridge on our left. We had problems, big problems. The caves had interlinking tunnels. We couldn't burn them out, or suffocate them with our flame-throwers.

We drove our tanks into Death Valley, hoping to take some of the pressure off the Infantry and onto us. Picking on targets of opportunity, we shot up a good number of the caves. One cave to our front fascinated me. The longer I stared at it through my periscope the more I began to identify the object of my intrigue. At the entrance or mouth of this cave, there was a man hanging from a rope attached to his neck. The body was severed at the waist. I told Harol about this cave and man. Harol could not locate the cave or man. I told him to look at his indictor to see where our 75 was aimed. Harol still could not locate the cave. I told Harol to move over and I stuck my head out of his hatch and looked. The tank crew always did think I was off my rocker, and this corroborated it. They thought their gunner had cracked up. I was hallucinating; there was no body there. Nothing was said, I was embarrassed, and the crew probably wondered, What's next?

With that behind us we went back to work. Harol wanted me to shoot up a rifle slit above and to the right of a cave opening. This sniper's hole was about ten inches in diameter. I fired an HE (high explosive) shell. Harol gave out with a scream... I turned and looked at him, he was holding his right shoulder. Pulling his fatigue shirt back, we saw his shoulder chopped up and bruised. I asked Harol if he was sticking his head out while I was shooting and he said yes. A little Army Corporal finally had his day. I chewed out a United States Army, a West Point graduate first lieutenant's ass... I barked at him, "I am pretty good with this gun but not that good! When I'm shooting pull your head inside the tank!" My round entered the rifle slot, nor cleanly, but ricocheting off the coral side. Harol got banged up with a chunk of coral. It wasn't that bad of a shot. I had to pinpoint a shell three inches in diameter into that firing slot at fifty yards.

We backed the tank out of the Valley to the area that the Infantry was working. They were calling it quits for the day so we drove to the usual dump, reloaded and gassed up. Returning to our outpost we set up a 30 caliber machine gun in the aperture of our sandbagged emplacement. While setting up our watches for our guard duty for the night Harol volunteered to take a shift. I wondered, seeing that Harol was going to live with us—the cannon fodder in the field—if he (Harol) wanted to become of the "boys". We gave Harol the first, the easy, watch of the night; that way hopefully he could get unbroken sleep. Our consideration was fruitless; while Ike was doing his watch, everyone was settled in and sleeping. We were roused from our peaceful sleep by the firing of a 30 caliber machine gun in our emplacement. Remember, we had a dependable crew and we enjoyed the luxury of sleep.

Ike let go with a series of short machine-gun bursts, and I asked Ike, "What's up?" Ike, in a quiet nonchalant voice, said, "That there's a Jap out there."

Remembering that Ike was a trained tank driver, and believing that Ike probably wanted to vent his anger or whatever by firing the gun, I said, "Okay, Ike, kill the son of a bitch and let's get some sleep." Laying there, I said to myself that there couldn't possibly be a Jap out there. When Lightning, Ike and I went out drinking beer at the PX, Ike always showed more emotion.

With Ike's firing of our machine gun, our sector received a lot of attention. The area was illuminated by a great amount of flares. Oddly enough there wasn't too much rifle fire or the explosion of grenades. My guess was that the Wildcats were battle-hardened and seasoned veterans, or maybe they just wanted to get some sleep.

At sunrise I left our sandbagged residence and gun emplacement for my morning toilet. Lo and behold, a freshly killed Jap was in front! Ike, a trained and excellent tank driver, had calmly and cool-headedly collected his first kill: good man, good job.

Last night's activity in our sector brought out the souvenir collectors and the ghouls, the scavengers. Two older "boys" appeared, and it was evident from their clean wearing apparel that they were probably second looeys, Headquarters personnel. We bullshitted and snow-jobbed them into buying our .45 caliber automatic side arms for fifty dollars each. The pencil-pushers were happy and Lightning and I were enriched with fifty dollars. Three sailors dressed in dungarees (blue denim work clothes) came a-looking. They headed straight for the mouth of the Valley. We yelled at them to get out and stay out of that area, they were under Jap fire. Two of the sailors backed off, the third, a stupid gob, yelled back at us to, "Blow it out of your ass, mate!"

This jerk then entered the Valley and started kicking teeth out of a skull. Apparently he was looking for the gold used to fill the cavities in the teeth. The retort of a Jap 25 caliber rifle was heard. Our "brave" scavenger, the asshole, cried out that he was hit, and then proceeded to moan, cry and beg for help.

We had to throw smoke grenades, and under the cover of this blanket of thick obscuring smoke, we pulled the son of a bitch out.

The Wildcats came up, and it was back to work.

Looking through my periscope, I watched the Infantry Team work. Under the guidance and direction of a GI, probably a Platoon

Sergeant, the Wildcats would give this man covering fire, he then would throw a fragmentation grenade into a cave, then set and detonate a satchel charge. This man was shot and killed in front of our tank while we watched. All work stopped. GIs then threw smoke and got his body out of there.

During the night the Jap had come out of the cave, hidden in a prepared rat's nest and concealed himself, waiting for this opportunity. But the Jap would pay the price.

Our tank was pulled back. Ike was told to get out to make room for a GI, who would pinpoint the location of the rat's nest and it's occupant. Ike, in evacuating, raised his seat in the high position, a position used when the drivers have their hatches open. With the seat in this position they have total vision in secure areas and it's much easier to climb out of the tank.

Our spotter, a six-footer with the physique of a professional football player, climbed up and into the tank. Settling down in Ike's seat, he dropped and secured his hatch. I looked down to where he was seated. This giant of a GI was doubled up and appeared to be in pain and very uncomfortable. I told Bill Weiss, our driver, to show him how to drop his seat by releasing the locking device. The Wildcat dropped his seat by releasing the locking device. The Wildcat dropped his seat turned and looked at me and said, "Thanks, buddy."

This man was probably very pleased and grateful that he was not assigned to a hot, cramped stinking iron coffin tank to do his bit. But, if he lives, he has his memories. When he is quaffing a few in his local Legion or VFW Post, he can now brag that he rode in a tightened up tank with a loaded 30 caliber machine gun in front of him.

Back to work: our GI pinpointed the rat's nest. Our troops now had one less Jap to contend with. But the caves that were worked over yesterday were now reoccupied and the Wildcats were sustaining casualties. Our tank and its 75 worked over the caves. Our assistance probably made the Jap mad and gave him a headache. Driving into the Valley, a live human, covered with coral dust, was a-top the China Wall, completely exposed in the skyline. He was throwing chunks of coral at our tank, probably aiming for Harol. I checked this being out with my periscope, then with my telescope. I still could not identify him as friend or foe. Harol told me not to kill him but to let him go.

Backing out of Death Valley to the mouth, our secured area, we were ordered to pick up American linguists, who by means of loudspeaker propaganda broadcasts were to try and persuade Colonel Nakagawa and his men surrender. Getting some fresh air and looking out of the turret hatch I saw a real rear-echelon dandy. This dude, an older person, probably a pencil-pushing Major (no escorting entourage) with his immaculate fatigues, was clean shaven and had well-shined shoes. He was out in the open by the right front side of the tank. I yelled down to him, "Mac, the Jap is out to your front, you're exposed, get under cover!"

I received a dirty look, but he obeyed and ducked under a coral ledge. I guess he came up to where the action was so he could claim that he was involved in the shooting war.

We picked up our passenger, bravely exposed on our rear engine deck. The linguist told the Japs in Japanese to lay down their arms and surrender; to die was senseless. Backing to our secured area, I proceeded to climb out of the turret, and coming out of the hatch I came face to face with a Jap. Bewildered, I almost fell backwards into the turret. Stunned, I regained my wits and realized that this man was on our side. He was the linguist from Intelligence!

After last night's activities, our sector received concertina (accordion-bellows type) rolls of barbed wire. These were brought up from the beach and stretched out by the entrance of Death Valley. We placed small pieces of coral into empty C-ration cans and then attached the cans to the springy barbed wire. We were now in business; any movement of the barbed wire would rattle the coral in the cans and we would be forewarned. The rear was looking out for us.

Our Company cooks donated a five-gallon can of fresh coffee grounds to the guys working the line. The First Sergeant was supposed to bring the coffee up. He told the Company maintenance men to bring it up to us. Everybody was afraid to visit us, and we never got our coffee; the mechanics drank it in the safety of the secured Company Base.

Our concertina was set up, now hopefully for some sleep; again we were to be denied a good night's rest. As with any group of young men, be it American or Japanese, there always is a character or characters.

I don't know how it started, but it began. Some Jap, slurring his "R"s, yelled, "Loosevelt sucki cocki!"

An American GI returned that communiqué with, "Tojo eats cunt!"

The Japs took offense with this communication and started shooting. We, being the foremost outpost, took the brunt of the Jap anger and frustration. The shooting finally stopped. We were glad; somebody could have gotten hurt, most likely us.

The morning found us making our daily excursion into the valley and shooting up targets of opportunity. Backing out and returning to our emplacement, we had the infrequent, very infrequent, experience of a Jap surrendering. The Jap was standing by the mouth of a cave to the rear of our emplacement. He was surrendering to our tank. I pointed the tank's cannon at him. Harol informed me, "Ed, if you kill him, they would court-martial me."

The Jap was told to strip. He was reasonably clean, uniform decent, and shaven. Standing in the heat of the tropical sun and quivering, understandably frightened and nervous. I dismounted from the tank and gave the Jap drinking water and a lit cigarette.

Humane? I doubt it, I believe it was to show the Japs in the caves that their game was lost. The Americans would treat them kindly, and it was now time to stop the slaughter of both American and Japanese cannon fodder, the wasting of good men.

Intelligence from Division Headquarters picked up our prize. We carried on with "our" war.

The day was spent harassing Japs by shooting up the caves, and making our presence felt. We expended a lot of ammo, two loads. The cave with the coral dam received about thirty shells, I tried ricocheting and skipping HE (like throwing flat stones on water). AP—armor-piercing shells—would not touch the dam. There were continual instances of caves being blown and declared secure, only to be reoccupied by the Japs within a short period of time. This whole procedure of blowing and burning caves would have to be repeated. The only solution to this cave problem was to search out and seal every opening in the coral mountainsides. The Jap positions were mutually supporting. The coral mountains, with their gullies, canyons and steep-sided fissures, provided Colonel Nakagawa's men with excellent defensive positions. Our Marines had paid, and the Wildcats were now to pay, a price—a helluva price—for this coral atoll.

The Umurbrogol Mountains, composed of solid coral, made it impossible to dig any protective foxholes. The best protection, later to be called an offensive weapon, was fifty pounds of sand enveloped in a burlap bag—the sandbag. All available rear echelon men, the scavengers and souvenir hunters, were put to work on this detail, filling sandbags. Now, as our troops captured the high ridges, they set up their protective sandbags, and then fortified these positions. The Wildcats were taking casualties, but they were also obtaining their objectives.

Attrition was taking its toll on Nakagawa's defenders. Now down to barely 350 combatants, Nakagawa sadly reported to General Inoue that he was unable to repulse the Americans with their successful usage of the sandbag. He was now rationing his ammunition and suffering a serious water shortage.

A short distance into Death Valley, and to the right, was a pass in the China Wall. Climbing this steep ridge into the pass, you enter the valley christened "Wildcat Bowl". The mountainous range of crests known as the "Five Brothers" separates the Wildcat Bowl from the "Horseshoe". This valley, about 250 yards long, shaped like a horseshoe, and about 100 yards at its widest girth, contained a freshwater pond, the source and supply of the Jap water. This basin containing the water was overlooked by the coral mountains of the Five Brothers to its west. To the east lay the Walt Ridge, the island's east road, and the ocean, with a boat dock and road entering the Walt Ridge.

The Wildcats came up, we joined them and went into the Horseshoe. Our tanks were emplaced beneath and alongside Walt Ridge, providing the Infantry with good protective fire. Our GIs went to work blowing and sealing the mouths of the caves. As the demolition charges were detonated in the Five Brothers, dust and smoke could be seen rising from Death Valley and the regions beyond. The Wildcats brought up their flame-thrower man. Man he has to be, and it must be emphasized: this GI, carrying jellied gasoline (napalm) in pressurized cylinder tanks, must go close, completely exposed to the enemy, and discharge from his tanks a stream of napalm which is ignited (hence flame-thrower) and hopefully enters the hot spot. His only protective friendly fire is from his concealed buddies who are providing covering fire. Our flame-thrower does an excellent job. He faces this cave and sends forth a stream of flaming napalm. He is on target: three Japs, uniforms burning, come running out of the cave screaming. The Infantry cuts them down with rifle fire. Another Jap, crazed, and probably drunk with saki, with his uniform smoldering and a bayonet attached to his rifle, makes a bonzai charge at our tanks.

When butchering chickens, the main artery in the chicken's neck is severed, and the chicken will run until its heart stops.

This Jap with his bayonet at the ready headed for our tanks. Our tank gunners laced this Jap's body up and down with 30 caliber projectiles from our machine guns. The Jap still come a-charging; he paused, then fell forward on his face. A dead Jap, his heart finally stopped like the butchered chicken.

After this slaughter of the Jap, you knew of and had to respect the fortitude of our enemy. You now wonder what is it going to be like when we invade his homeland, the islands that compose the Japanese nation...

Our flame-thrower took one, he was probably shot by a hidden sniper. His tank was ruptured exploded and burned. What a hell of a way for a good man to go out.

The GIs called it quits for the day. We pulled back to our station at the mouth of Death Valley. This Wildcats left their bowl, the Wildcat Bowl, through the pass, and returned to their base. We, with our tanks and the Infantry, did not draw any fire during the process of evacuation.

Our nightly guard was established and posted. We settled down for what was hopefully a good night. We had one. All was quiet and peaceful, our sector did not even draw any flares. We were allowed our dreams and got some rest.

Sunrise found everything serene, we had our lukewarm instant coffee and consumed our breakfast; the egg portion of our combat rations food supply. Our spam and pineapple were long gone.

We were now faced with another day. This new-found serenity on this island, Peleliu, was perplexing. We were slightly bewildered and puzzled—where was the Jap? Then the Infantry came up and entered the pass leading into the Bowl and the Horseshoe. All hell broke loose; continued and rapid fire, rifle fire, came from the Horseshoe. We got our tank ready to move out and assist the Infantry, but they never called upon us. After a bit, the Wildcats emerged. As they passed, we mentioned that it sounded like you guys declared war. What was going on? The Wildcats stated that they were shooting at each other—no casualties. Our Wildcats left our sector without drawing any Jap fire.

Lightning and I decided it was time to reconnoiter. We went to the right rear side of Old Baldy to where the mouth of a cave was located, the same cave our prize the Jap emerged from and surrendered to us.

There they were, the rotten and stinking bodies of the dead Japs. We heard the hum of thousands of large blue-black flies hovering over and feasting upon the decomposed bodies. The tropical heat had bloated the bodies. Some of the dead Japs had their mouths and eyes open, the open eyes glaring at you as only the dead can glare. The open mouths on some revealed glittering gold fillings in their teeth caught by the sunlight. The flies were landing on the eyeballs and going into the open mouths. Some of the bloated bellies were laid open, and the expanded bowels and guts were exposed. Maggots scurried in and out feasting on the rotting flesh.

With the lack of combat noise and activity, we gained a degree of bravado. We entered this large cave. The ledges that the Jap had chiseled out of the coral for sniper activity above and to the sides of the mouth of the cave were visible. To the rear, in the dark hallows of the cave we heard it: the clicking of metal striking a hard object. We got out of that cave in a hurry and scurried to the side of the cave's entrance. The coral walls of the Five Brothers mountain peaks would protect us from any exploding grenades. But no explosion. This inspired us and gave us some gumption, we started looking into other caves, not entering, just looking. A cave in the China Wall contained what appeared to be the treasure that we were seeking.

There it was, inside and to the right of the cave opening; a small jewel-type box of highly polished, beautiful teak wood gleaming in the dim sunlight that was illuminating the cave's entrance. Our desired treasure—did it contain gold? Valuable and highly prized precious stones? We were soon to find out. But… there was one drawback. Our desired and hoped-for treasure was dust free. Having dealt with the Jap, and knowing of his diabolic and devious ways, we would not enter the cave and liberate this obvious treasure. The signs indicated that it was possible and very probable that our treasure was booby-trapped. We did not have any objects such as grappling hooks to dislodge and move that box, believing that it was possible that there could be a dynamite charge underneath. Another factor we had to take into consideration was that it was very possible that our treasure chest contained explosives to be detonated upon opening the box.

It was decided that the detonation of a concussion grenade would possibly cause a booby-trap to explode. That was our new approach and course to pursue. We pulled the safety pin out of a concussion grenade, activated the grenade's firing by releasing the safety handle, counted three fast seconds, then threw the grenade into and to the right of the area of our treasure. We waited another three fast seconds and our grenade exploded… no additional explosions. We still lacked the guts (maybe it was good sense) to retrieve our treasure. We left our dream of wealth for the scavengers.

Back in the Horseshoe, the process of attrition continued. The Engineers Unit of the Wildcat Division mounted floodlights to focus on the freshwater pond, thereby depriving the Jap of his water source. They rigged up a flame-thrower, a 300-yard pipeline from a fuel truck parked on the West Road, complete with booster pumps to insure pressure. Now the flame-thrower operator could play his flame on Japanese positions like water from a hose. The 306th Engineering Battalion built ramps for our tanks. They developed conveyor systems to get supplies up into the ridges and to evacuate the wounded.

On November 13, supporting the Infantry, we were ordered into the Wildcat Bowl. Our second looey, known as Caffin, took command of Harol's tank, Champagne. Caffin took charge. He directed us into the pass leading into the Wildcat Bowl. Entering and taking a position in the Bowl, Caffin, through the use of the indicator, aimed by verbal command the 75 at the coral mountain range known as the Five Brothers. Caffin then inquired as to how many rounds I had. I told him about a hundred rounds. Caffin then ordered me to shoot them up and then we'd get the hell out of there. The coral mountain that Caffin had aimed my gun at was solid coral—no caves, firing holes or even crevasses. I started picking my own targets, firing and getting rid of our ammo. After firing about ten rounds, I had difficulty breathing. Bill, our driver, and his assistant, Ike, were coughing. I looked at Lightning who was loading the 75; the sharpie had his porthole open wide and he was getting air. I turned and looked at Caffin directly behind me. His hatch was closed and secured. I told the Lieutenant to open the hatch and to get some air into the tank. Assuming that Caffin had obeyed my directive, I went back to expending our ammo. I received a tap on my shoulder, and there was Caffin pointing at an ink marking on his shoulder that designated a looey's bar on his shoulder. He then stated that he was in charge of this tank, and did we want him to get killed?

I told Caffin that somebody spilt ink on his shoulder, and he should open his hatch.

After firing a few more rounds, the cordite fumes of the explosives filled the turret, and we did not have any oxygen to breathe. Caffin still had his hatch closed and locked. I then told Caffin, "You yellow son of a bitch! You aren't going to kill this crew! You bastard, if you do not open your hatch, I shall throw you out of the tank and you can run back to the beach. You are no longer commanding this tank and crew. Keep your fucking mouth shut and open your hatch!"

I then got up from my seat and unlocked and opened the hatch. I told Bill to start the tank's engine and get some air circulating inside.

Lightning then took over as the tank's Gunner; I did the loading for him. Lightning was pinpointing and hitting designated targets. His gunnery was excellent, and it could have put a few, quite a few, of the Company's Gunners to shame. Lightning shot up and got rid of the remaining 75 ammo and then we sat and waited. There was a banging of coral against the back of the tank and some yelling. I pushed Caffin aside and looked out of the hatch. There was this distraught GI, no weapon, lacking a helmet and the other prescribed equipment. He begged me for an M1 (Garand rifle). I climbed out of the tank and, placing my hands on his shoulders, I eased him to the back of the tank, out of harm's way. He sobbingly told me that his buddy got killed and he wanted to go up there (hills) and kill the sons of bitches. I gently told him that we would take care of the Japs and ordered him to return to his unit. Crying, he walked away from the danger area and proceeded to the beach. We also left the Wildcat Bowl and returned to our base.

The next day Harol resumed command. The Infantry entered the Bowl and started working over the caves. They detonated demolition charges at cave entrances. Where that failed to block the caves, the mouths or entrances were sealed with concrete.

Our sandbags, the denial to the Jap of his water source, and the continual pressure by the Wildcats, were becoming highly successful. The enemy was being driven and compressed into the Walt Ridge pocket, south of the Horseshoe and off the East Road, where the Jap had his boat dock and stored Naval supplies in the caves of Walt Ridge.

The pattern of victory was shaping up for the final kill. Hitting the Walt Ridge pocket, the Infantry stopped at the outer fringes and started taking casualties. The push stopped and a GI, probably the Infantry's Unit Commander, called for a napalm air strike. He threw smoke grenades, and under this concealing smoke went out and laid a signifying panel. This panel was a guide for the bomber pilots to drop their napalm bombs to the front of the panel and into the pocket. The shortest bomb run in the Pacific Theater was developing. The bombers were loaded with napalm at the airstrip just off the Umurbrogol Mountains. Their bomb run was just 1,000 yards away! Because of the close proximity of the Infantry Unit working the pocket, the igniters were removed from the napalm bombs. The bomber pilot dropped his napalm on target in the pocket and returned to the airstrip. The Infantry Mortar Team laid phosphorous shells on the napalm. We now had a raging inferno in the pocket. The fire subsided, but the heated coral from the napalm was too hot to do any work. We returned to base. Lightning and I had no sooner alighted from the tank than our First Sergeant was upon us. He told us that we were on guard duty that night. I faced the Sergeant and said, "What?" He repeated his order; we were on guard duty. I then proceeded to tell the First Sergeant that we were not sitting on our asses on the line jerking ourselves off, he had the crews of five disabled tanks and his Headquarters Platoon and could put them on guard duty; we were pulled back to get some rest. The whistle-happy jerkey Sergeant told us that Luzinas and Kern were next on the roster. We were on guard duty.

Lt. Harol listened and observed this heated discussion. He would not step on the Sarge's toes nor would he support his tank crew. Harol turned his back on the issue and walked away.

We drove the tank to the sentry outpost and settled in for the night, Lightning and I alternating a two-hour guard, then a two and a half-hour sleep shift.

As the tropical sun was starting to set, I heard the whispered call, "Luzinas… Luzinas." I stuck my head out of the tank's turret and looked down. There was Lt. Caffin pointing a Colt 45 caliber automatic side arm at my head. He asked if Lightning and I were going out tomorrow. I knew that we would not go hunting tomorrow, and decided to play the game. I told Caffin that I was tired, I would see how Lightning felt. Checking with Lightning inside the turret, he gave me the same, that he would go along with my decision, whatever it was. I stuck my head out of the turret and told Caffin that we were tired, check with us in the morning. Kicking this around, we assumed that Lt. Harol was taking another day off, probably because he knew that we would not go out.

Being in the rear and in the secured area we had a quiet and peaceful night, but we still had to contend with our broken sleep. At sunrise and in good light, there he was—Caffin—with his Colt 45 pointing at my head and asking if we were going out today. I told Caffin that we were tired, damned tired, and that we were going to take the day off and get some rest.

At that time it was an enjoyable decision, but one that we would regret.

Lightning and I took the day off. We reconnoitered the White

Beach area by Dead Man's Curve. The beach was littered with burned and shot up landing craft, equipment and the debris that is found on a beachhead. In our search we did not find anything that we considered valuable. The Jap sniper of Dead Man's Curve did not lay any fire on us; the Wildcats had probably caught up with him. Returning to our base, we got the bad news. A good man, a First Platoon Buck Sergeant, a tank commander, got killed working the Walt Ridge Pocket. We were notified that a sniper got him in the back. Our man was too conscientious, he had his head and shoulders out of the turret, surveying his front through binoculars. Apparently he was emulating his Platoon Leader, Harol. A valiant man who gave up his life needlessly. We wondered, where was Caffin? He as the officer and leader was the point tank. What was a Buck Sergeant doing as point?

We had a day off, then it was back to work. It was now our turn to go into the Pocket.

Entering the Pocket area we found the 306th Engineers hard at work in the coolness of the morning, striving to assemble a "snake" before the unbearable and prostrating heat of the equator took its toll.

This "snake" being assembled was composed of numerous Bangalore Torpedoes. The Bangalore Torpedo, a piece or length of pipe filled with explosives, was used to clear and detonate land mines etc.

Our orders came through. Our tank was to be used to ease and or snake the lengthy piping of Torpedoes into the Pocket. Because the "snake" was made of tons of explosives we would have to remove all munitions from the tank, leaving just a belt of 30 caliber for the machine gun. The "snake" upon being positioned in the Pocket would be ignited and explode by our tank firing its 30 and hitting a bullseye, which was to be located at the tail end—our end—of the "snake".

Our day was spent watch-dogging the Engineers as they sweated, manhandling the explosives.

A few "incidents" did happen that are worthy of mention.

To the left of the sweating Wildcats and at the edge of the mouth of the pocket, the Japs had positioned a naval Torpedo, the type used in submarines to destroy sea-going vessels. Our tank crew, being curious, investigated. After a cursory examination we left.

The Jap had a few tricks to accomplish at his final stand before he fulfilled his destiny, which was to die honorably for his Emperor.

An amplified bellow, an electrifying shriek sent all present hitting the ground, shivering, expecting who knows what. Some GIs soiled their pants. The Jap probably smiled and smirked. That was it! On a knoll that was out of the Engineer's way, we came upon a couple of GIs. I looked at one of them and was shocked. I thought, Our country is in trouble, big trouble… Facing me, and I thinking he was a draftee, was a GI who appeared to be about fifty years of age with silvery gray hair appearing from underneath his helmet. I said to myself that our country must really be short of manpower to grab cannon fodder this old. My assumptions were incorrect; this old timer was a Commander of the Infantry Unit, he was waiting for his troops. They never arrived.

We proceeded in unloading our ammo by shooting it up at targets of opportunity. When that was completed we returned to base. For the first time on these islands we did not go to the ammo dump to reload and restock the tank. I guess this was supposed to be a breather for the things which were to come on the following day. The Wildcats must have got their asses chewed. Mid-morning we received word—no work today.

The Wildcats got to the Pocket early. While waiting for their tank support they had looked over the Japanese naval torpedo: fourteen killed outright and twenty-four wounded. The Jap laughed at that one. He had the torpedo booby-trapped. The Jap apparently did not think that the crew of the tank Champagne was worth the price of a naval torpedo. Thank God he did not set it off yesterday while we were looking at it, we thought.

A hell of a price was paid by the Wildcats for a day off. But attrition and the continuous Wildcat pressure on the Jap was paying off. We did not return to the Pocket to blow the snake.

During the night of November 24–25, the Japs emerged from the caves. Forty-five of the Jap were killed, including two officers. It was the end of the Japs' organized resistance. A captured Jap prisoner's story and account was that Colonel Nakagawa and Major General Kenjire Maurai had ordered this attack to break through American lines and to conduct guerilla warfare against the occupied areas. The

Regimental Colors were then burned in the military tradition of the Japanese, signifying that the Regiment ceased to exist and should be stricken from the Army lists. The Jap officers then notified Headquarters that the end had come. They then ceremoniously shot themselves. Throughout the day of November 25, thirty more Japs were flushed out as the Wildcats searched with infinite care to make sure that not a single Jap was overlooked. Twenty-one more were killed during the night in what appeared to be individual attempts to escape to other islands. November 26 was a repetition of the previous day, with resistance still encountered at the head of Death Valley.

The assaulting units jumped off in all areas of resistance on November 27. Elements of the Second Battalion moved northward along the China Wall and were joined by the Wildcats of the Third Battalion who were working southward. Across the intervening yardage they could see the men of the First Battalion perched on the rim of Death Valley. Resistance to this many-sided attack seemed to disintegrate completely. For long moments the weary Wildcats looked at each other in welcome silence, trying to realize and realizing that this was all there was: there wasn't any more.

At 1100 hours, Colonel Arthur P. Watson, commanding the 323 Regimental Combat Team, reported to General Mueller that the Peleliu operation was over.

"The Enemy had fulfilled his determination to fight to the Death."

14: The Palaus in Retrospect

Early in September, Admiral Halsey's carriers pounded the Palaus. In the September 6–8 period, bombers and fighters from three carrier groups swept back and forth over the islands. They encountered practically no opposition. Some of the escort cruisers and destroyers even bombarded Angaur and Peleliu. Admiral Halsey next turned his forces and attention to the Philippines. He found Jap opposition weak, surprisingly weak. On September 13, Admiral Halsey recommended to Admiral Nimitz that a number of preliminary operations, including the Palaus, be dropped in order to invade the Central Philippines immediately. Ulithi was to be seized as a fleet anchorage; the rest of the Stalemate 11 operation was cancelled and assigned troops could then be freed to reinforce the landings in the Philippines.

Whether General Douglas MacArthur could have invaded the Philippines successfully with the Palaus in Japanese control is a matter of speculation. MacArthur did not think so at the time; neither did Admiral Nimitz, nor the Joint Chiefs of Staff.

The United States forces hit the Palau beaches, the US Marines Peleliu, on September 15.

The United States Army invaded Angaur on September 17.

The die was cast, for better or worse. MacArthur's flank was secured, and the Pacific War entered into a new and decisive phase. That doubt should be cast on the strategic importance of the Palaus and their seizure is debasing to the memory of the men who fought and died there.

Victory did not come cheap. The Official US Army History of the campaign describes it as one of the bloodiest battles of the war.

The First Marines and support units had 1,252 killed and missing, with 5,274 wounded.

The US Army's 81st Division, with attached units, had 542 dead and 2,736 wounded.

A total of nearly 10,000 American Casualties.

Almost 1,800 killed and missing; 8,000 wounded.

A hell of a lot of good men. Both the Japs and Americans paid the price for the doubtful value of Japanese real estate, the Palau Islands.

The Palau Campaign ended on November 27, 1944—two and a half months after it began.

What we Americans gained with this expensive coral: a large Japanese Force was isolated; General Inoue and some 25,000 Japanese remained on Babelthaup and other nearby Islands, by-passed, cut off and unable to interfere with our operations. There they remained until the Japanese nation surrendered.

The Palau Campaign in hindsight remains one of the tragic costs of the war; unnecessary, but perhaps certain to happen. No one can state in full certainty what would have happened had the Stalemate 11 Campaign not taken place.

What is known is that the air facilities on Peleliu and then those developed on Angaur proved useful as staging and support for the Philippines Campaign. The Jap was denied the whole of the Palau Island chain as a base for attacking our shipping and the lines of communication supporting the Philippines Invasion.

15: New Caledonia A French Paradise

Fate was kind to us in the Palaus. She let us live, and gave us revelations of things we could expect in battles upcoming,

On December 8 we boarded transports and set sail for the French island possession, New Caledonia, to lick our wounds and to undergo the Army's precept of the "R"s. We left the island of Peleliu in the capable hands of occupation troops to mop up and eliminate the Jap stragglers.

The Army's "R"s—and there are a good many of them—meant Refitted-Retrained-Reorganized, and hopefully, Rest and Recreation. The best GIs "R" is relaxation. This we commenced doing on our cruise to New Caledonia, an island 8,548 miles square in area in the South-western Pacific Ocean, about 800 miles east of Australia.

Our Navy resumed the gun watches. The only duties assigned to the Army were in the galley, assisting the Navy chefs in preparing the excellent Navy chow and the clean-up that followed.

This new-found freedom allowed us to unwind from the tensions and stress of existing and hopefully living under the eyes and weaponry of the Japs.

A great deal of time was devoted to re-evaluating and qualifying the kids we trained with back in Polk, Louisiana. The "kids" were no longer boys or recruits, they had received their baptism of fire and stood up in time of war. No longer were they glassy eyed, and believing in the glorification of war as portrayed by the Hollywood movie industry. These "boys" had seen and participated in the true agonies of war. They were aghast at war's horror, yet they had proved their mettle.

Of course every "boy" did not develop or prove himself as a man in stressful situations. One of the noticeable ones in our platoon was the Buck Sergeant Alvin, Commander of the fourth tank in line. During training, Alvin was a brown-nosing asshole, boasting and implying that he, Alvin, would be a stand-out killer. In combat he reverted back to his true self; a church mouse.

As was to be expected, other "leaders" were raked over the coals. We laughed over the bragging kids who kissy-kissy assed for promotions that the table of organizations called for in training. These self-styled "leaders" in combat entered into quiet seclusion, wishing they could bury their heads in a hole in the ground like an ostrich, but knowing if they proceeded with this tactic their butts would be exposed and protruding upwards. The men, the Privates, would then enjoy kicking a few asses. We were in complete agreement that three of our Company Officers were clowns and should be avoided. Our Platoon Sergeant held up well. The Sergeant who scored the most brownie points was Karle, the Commander of the second tank in line, our back-up tank. Karle, always a quiet reserved man stood up well under enemy fire and did not get shook. Sergeant Karle; a good man, good job.

Other details are worthy of mention. The men no longer congregated. They were now separate, usually two to four buddies in each group. Their casual and friendly banter was missing. I guess it was the Japs who changed our "boys" into men with the realization that they were cannon fodder with a highly questionable life existence.

Life must go on: we began to look forward to our reprieve and what we hoped would be a joyful, quiet sojourn on a French island. I guess we were looking for or dreaming of the French girls and their can-can dancing. But... the battle was over. The shit-heels with their stripes and authority came out of hiding and started throwing their rank around. I believe that in combat these "heroes" were afraid of taking a friendly, but deadly, hit that would wipe them out. How soon they, the "heroes", forget that another invasion and battle was on the horizon.

After doing the job we were trained for (and I must brag a bit on doing it well, without the Army and its chicken-shit riding on our backs), we were told that we were still in the Army.

The Army then resumed providing it with their highly questionable methods. As we steamed into our new port o'call, the harbor of Noumea—the Capital of New Caledonia—I was reminded of our landing in the Hawaiian Islands. The Army then informed us naive kids that if we ate fresh pineapple our teeth would rot. Here, in this French paradise, the Army attempted a new tack. We were told that booze (whiskey) would blind us. The available French women were either clapped or syphed up.

As soon as we were tied up at the wharf and our gangway lowered, a Military Policemen, armed, assumed sentry duty. We were prisoners aboard ship.

The Army snow-jobbed us kids in Hawaii, and now they were attempting the same shit with battle-hardened veterans. To reinforce their directive, they kept us under armed guard.

We departed from Pearl Harbor, Hawaii, on August 8, 1944. At sea and existing on the islands for four months, we were then brought back to the world and civilization. The Army tells us that there are women and booze on this beautiful but primitive island. We were virile young men being denied by the methods and madness of our Army and an armed guard; then again, that could very possibly be the intent and purpose of the brass.

We were told to be ready to disembark the following day. We would then journey to our new camp, Camp Ritchie. Lightning and I spent the day at the rail of the ship, looking at the small community—backward by our standards—of Noumea. There was the French Tricolor flag flying above the harbor. A wooden weather-stained church was located on a rise overlooking the harbor. The only activity to be seen ashore involved military personnel, probably stationed there as part of General MacArthur's staff of his Designated south-west Pacific Sector. New Caledonia was a crucial staging center in the early stages of the war, but the conflict has moved on, heading for Japan proper, and now in the Philippines.

Yearning to get ashore and enjoy whatever treasures or pleasures that Noumea could bestow, we agreed: nothing ventured, nothing gained. As we were walking down the gangway, the MP stopped us and demanded to see our passes. Not having passes, we did not get ashore. But we bullshitted with the MP. We tried negotiating for a bottle of whiskey. We were informed that there was a limited supply of American whiskey which was the officers' rations and it was very, very expensive. Some Australian whiskey was available, but it was very difficult to come by and expensive.

Inquiring about the French girls and women, we were told to stop dreaming. They were sheltered, and only seen with their parents present.

He told us about "The Pink House", a government-sponsored and controlled cat house, that "serviced" the troops. No luck; we could not get ashore, so we spent the balance of the day dreaming.

After morning chow we moved out to our new camp located in the boondocks, miles away from Noumea.

We were in the Army again.

In combat a GI has to think for himself and do for himself if he is to live and survive. Orders from Brass were limited. Here in camp the regimentation began. Yes, we were back in the Army; the First Sergeant reappeared with his police whistle, and the chicken-shit began.

It started with the army's version of recreation. Orders specified that all available personnel shall comply. We were to proceed to our Red Cross Rehabilitation Camp and "enjoy" a donut and coffee while we were resting.

A good day in a French paradise wasted.

Then we became involved in the process of getting refitted. We were told to turn in all worn-out wearing apparel and equipment for replacement. I was doing fine; the Supply, a Staff Sergeant, accepted my Garand rifle (MI Infantry Personal Weapon) which I turned in to replace and cover my missing Thompson sub-machine gun. No questions. I requested and ordered a new barrel for our tank's 75 MM cannon. It being a strange requisition, he questioned it. I told him to check his daily record of rounds fired, and that would reaffirm this requisition and show that the spiral grooves cut into the barrel of the cannon to obtain accuracy when fired were worn down. This cannon was no longer an artillery piece; it was now a mortar.

Next came requisitions for shoes, fatigues and underwear: no problem. But the Supply Sergeant started throwing his rank at me when I ordered new canvas leggings to cover the loss of the ones I cut up and used as ankle supports. He stated that leggings were not used in this campaign and that I had destroyed Government property, and demanded that I sign a statement of charges to cover the cost of the leggings. I looked him in the eye and told him to cut it out with the shit and check with the Old Man (Commanding Officer of the

Company). The CO had directed and authorized this makeshift ankle support so I could be available and fit to go to war. The Supply Sergeant then backed off and I did not have any further problems with him. It is laughable. No question was raised about the loss of my personal weapon, the tommy-gun and it being replaced— replaced by the MI, which was easily obtained at the Salvage Yard, that is, the Army.

The United States and its military forces have always awarded men who distinguish themselves in battle. Our Battalion was now to participate and follow in this established and honored ceremony.

Duffel bags with our personal belongings and uniforms caught up to us. Orders of the Day were: dress in suntans (summer uniforms), hats and shirts minus ties, pants, and pistol belts. Then, march to the parade grounds in full Battalion force with the Battalion Band.

A full dress parade, with an eyes right salute to the Honored Recipients and the presenting Brass.

The dedication begins with the Brass and their line of crap. Then the awarding of the Medals—some deserving, others highly questionable, and it made one wonder how far our military and its system has decayed with this deceit. Headquarter Officers whose only knowledge of front-line combat and activity came out of what they had seen in movies were being awarded Silver and Bronze Stars. Technician Fifth Grade Ollie, our tank's Radio Man and Leader, was honored with the presentation of the Bronze Star; his award should have been the Silver Star—Ollie earned it.

Our Tank Commander, Lieutenant Harol, had been wounded in the right shoulder but did not even receive a Purple Heart. However, Lt. Harol was rewarded, or awarded—whatever the case may be— with a promotion. A Company Commander of our Battalion flipped (had a mental breakdown) and Harol was given a new assignment: Company Commander and a promotion to Captain.

With the loss of Harol and Ollie, and the absence of our Assistant Driver, that left our tank's driver Bill and I as being the last of the stateside crew of the real United States Army Tank C5 710th Tank Battalion.

Taking my canteen containing water, a can of hash and my fork and also my stationery, I went deep into the woods back of our encampment to reflect and attempt to create an analysis of my present predicament—the Army. While in meditation I sensed that I was being observed. I cautiously looked up, there was a deer observing me. Yes, a real live deer, a beautiful deer. We stared at each other for a few moments, then I foolishly moved and my companion took off.

That loveable animal made me realize that I would have to undertake more senseless killing of my fellow human beings, and probably give up my life in turn.

Life is still beautiful and valuable, even though it contains and envelops a lot of grief. Our grief was soon to come. We now had to train the new officer who was to command our tank, and teach and break in two new crew members. Our borrowed stalwarts, Lightning and Ike, proven, trusting and dependable, excellent *men* to go to war with, were irreplaceable, and now we were forced to deal and fight a war with the misfits and outcasts from a repple depple (Replacement Center). When the Company received its new tanks replacing ones lost in combat, Lightning and Ike would have to return to Karle's Tank. Dammit, they most certainly would be missed.

Our American forces had turned the tide in the Pacific. Our island-hopping and the staging areas were now paying off. We were now about to rest and gain a foothold in the islands that the Japanese considered as her protective ring in the defense of her homeland.

General MacArthur's Forces hit and landed on the island of Leyte in the Philippines on October 20, 1944, fulfilling the General's pledge that he would return.

We, back at New Caledonia, started preparing for our next adventure, if you wish to call war that.

The boys that were of no use to our unit were shipped out to Replacement Centers. A Platoon Sergeant (Staff) was relieved of his responsibility and demoted to Buck Sergeant and made Company Armorer, a rear echelon job. Our Company conducted its critique, a critical and thorough examination of our recent experiences in battle. Our moderator, a Company officer, chewed us out in a nice way and started an enumeration of faults committed. After listening to his complaints and whining, a college educated GI got the floor and agreed with the officer. He stated, yes, we have made a hell of a lot of mistakes. We would never learn, so the obvious solution was—surrender and go home. The body of men took this as a motion. It was seconded and voted upon. The vote was unanimous: let's surrender and go home! Our moderator, a real killjoy, dissented. He told us we were in the Army and to take orders and not give them. Our spokesman was applauded for his effort.

The next notable and heart-rending event to be experienced was our first Christmas overseas.

As the darkness of the night blanketed our area on Christmas Eve, the only sounds to be heard were those of the frogs croaking, and those made by our cooks working in the illumination that was created by gasoline lanterns. The silence was sickening, unlike the normal bullshitting of young men. These may have been battle-hardened veterans but they were still kids at heart. Many a pillow must have been wet by the tears that were shed by these "kids" as they thought of home and their loved ones back in the States.

Out of the silence of the night came the sound of joy. "*Silent night, holy night...*" someone was singing Christmas Carols. The camp picked up on this and sang carols.

The holiday tension was eased. Our cooks were up and working all night under adverse, very adverse, conditions in the field. With the use of gasoline stoves they prepared a good dinner, the Army's traditional Christmas dinner of turkey and the trimmings; even pumpkin pie.

The men of our unit thanked our cooks for their effort and the results of their efforts—a good meal.

It being the Christmas Holidays, Lightning and I were to be reassured that there is a Santa Claus with presents.

The Army's Island Command notified our Battalion of roughly nine hundred men, which was the composition of our unit, that they authorized two men from our unit to be sent to the Army's Special Services Camp for four days of rest and recreation.

Lightning and I were selected. We entered this place of heaven in the South Pacific. A country club environment with all the luxuries of civilian life. A bar with what was to be our private bartender and a plentiful supply of excellent Australian beer. Our barkeep told us that

Brass (Officers) was not allowed in this camp, and any expression of rank was forbidden. We were presented with a written agenda and camp rules.

Breakfast:	8 A.M. to 11:30 A.M.
Lunch:	12 noon to 3 P.M.
Dinner:	4:30 P.M. to 8 P.M.

…with a special thank-you from the Army and orders to enjoy our stay at camp. Being *good soldiers*, we had to obey this Army Directive, as we were the pick of the litter. We consumed a quantity of excellent Australian beer and conferred with our barkeep, who befriended and advised us. Breakfast was at our convenience and we enjoyed specially prepared-as-ordered foods from a menu. A GIs dream, being served by cute waitresses offering juices, fresh eggs, and fresh milk in abundance at a round dining-room table with real chairs, not benches.

After breakfast we roamed around and got familiar with Noumea and its surroundings.

Lunch was buffet style: salads, thinly sliced beef, ham and turkey, cheeses and fruit.

Now, our *dinners* were something to write home about.

Salad with Roquefort cheese, yet Roquefort cheese dressing. Thick succulent prime beef steaks flavored and broiled to order. Real potatoes creamed, fruit and French pastries. After an early dinner we would enjoy the sights and pleasures that French Noumea could and did provide.

After floating on cloud nine and being a civilian for four days, the Army broke our bubble. A truck came to pick us up. Our barkeep buddy thanked us and wished us good luck and then gave us a bottle of Australian whiskey. Our driver and his truck then returned us to the real United States Army.

As soon as the truck dropped us off at base, Bill gave us the word that our new Tank Commander, a second looey from the Officer's Pool, had joined our Company. Bill said our new officer was a Regular Army enlisted man who was commissioned at the outbreak of hostilities. We asked Bill what he thought of Lieutenant William

Kambell. "When you see him, judge for yourself," was Bill's reply. Lightning and I now had the pleasant job of relaying our experiences and doings at the Rand R Camp to the rest of our platoon. We laid it on heavy, let the poor slobs eat their hearts out!

That evening, after obtaining beer from our PX, we and our own little clique from the tank Champagne retired to the privacy of our tent and drank boiler makers (booze and beer) and had a good bullshit session. The war and the Army with all of its crap was not the crux of our discussions.

The next morning after chow, having a slight hangover, I went out and there he was, Second Lieutenant Kambell, a pear-shaped individual about thirty-three years old and five feet six inches tall, overweight with a pot belly. His stature and the way he wore his fatigues were that of a sad sack and not that of the elite, the officers. My first impression and thoughts were that we were in trouble, big trouble. Like a puppy-dog, "Soup" (Kambell) followed his crew around, snooping and brown-nosing. He was trying to be one of the boys, but also letting us know that he was an officer. Yes siree, there was trouble a-brewing on the far horizon.

We began extensive training for our next assignment and campaign, Okinawa, as reserves. We improved our tank infantry team techniques. The use of our tanks as mobile artillery was stressed and developed. In the Palaus we fired on and destroyed targets that were visible to the gunners at short ranges. Our new training indicated large mass warfare and long-range artillery firing. While firing, our tank being the center point or target-finding gun, with our periscopes dropped with vision, simulating artillery firing on long-range unseen targets. I misread a compass heading on our Azimuth Indicator by ten degrees. I found the target with our central gun. The five tanks of our platoon were then ordered to fire their spread on the designated target areas, with the spreading being equal to the distance separating our tanks. The first gun on our left fired. Bill, our Driver, looking out through his periscope told me that our gun was not in line, that I was off. I cheated, raised my periscope and watched the burst of the second tank on my left. Indeed, I was off so I quickly made my correction and fired. The two tanks on our right fired. Our five-gun spread was proper; the target area (though not as planned) was covered, a little slightly to the left, but covered. Not a word was said; just think, if I hadn't leveled the bubble in my quadrant and dropped a short round, I might have wiped out the OP (observation post) with all the Brass!

In our outfit—as it is in the rest of the Army—the Private is always handed the cruddy, or better known as the shitty, end of the stick—and he has to take it.

The men of our unit had ingenuity; they reserved the Army's method and passed the buck or responsibility back to the Brass and gained and hopefully enjoyed some intoxicating beer to boot for their creativity.

As Corporal of the Guard I posted my sentinels and returned to the guard tent. The alarm came—"Corporal of the Guard!" Grabbing my tommy-gun, I went to investigate. The man guarding the PX with its treasured beer reported the theft of some cases of beer. I called the next in line, the Sergeant of the Guard, and he in turned called the Officer of the Day. Returning to the guard tent, I wondered how my watchman and his buddies were going to chill their beer... or were they going to enjoy it warm?

Late in the year of 1944, a long-range bomber, the B29 Superfortress, a plane twice the size of any bombers then in use, lifted off the Boeing Aircraft runway. This battleship of the skies, sixty-five tons of shining silver with a range of 3,500 miles and capable of carrying a four-ton bomb load, needed a base.

At the time of the Marianas Campaign, June 15, 1944, the Army had five hundred fully manned B-29s. The Mariana Islands—Tinian, Saipan, and Guam—were roughly fourteen hundred miles from Tokyo. They were ideally suited to serve as a base for these magnificent birds. A safe secure haven or fall-back was needed for the Superforts' Fighter Escort and to render service for the crippled and damaged bombers on their flights to the Japanese homeland and return after their bomb runs.

Nampo Shoto was a chain of islands off the southern coastline of Japan. They formed the volcano group of islands of which one, Iwo Jima, was en route from the Marianas to the Japanese homeland. Iwo Jima is an island roughly seven hundred miles from Tokyo, and seven hundred miles from the Marianas. A total of fourteen hundred miles, well inside the Superfortress's range of three thousand and five hundred miles with its four-ton bomb load. Iwo Jima, an island centrally located and large enough to support a bomber strip and a strip for the P51s, their fighter escort, was our target.

The team assigned for this job was as follows:

The Fourth Marine Division—The Fifth Marine Division

In Reserve—The Third Marine Division

Objective: The island of Iwo Jima

The Marine Assault Forces totaled 70,647 men.

The Army garrison and Navy men on shore duty were an additional force of 111,308 men. With the Naval forces of the ships involved added in, the entire force totaled over a quarter of a million men.

On February 19, 1945, the Marines landed on Iwo. Another bloodbath: United States Marines and US Navy casualties included 5,931 killed or died of wounds and another 17,272 wounded.

Of the Japanese, 216 were taken prisoner out of a garrison of 22,000; about 21,784 men killed.

But we now had an emergency landing field for our B29s, which were pounding the Japanese homeland.

On Easter Sunday, April 1, 1945, four US Divisions of our fighting forces established a beachhead on Okinawa in our island-hopping steps to the Japanese homeland. Okinawa, 350 miles from Japan, is the largest island in the Ryukyu chain of islands. Landing, after Naval preparation, were the Sixth and the First Marines and the Seventh and Ninety-sixth Army Infantry divisions, which composed the Tenth Army under Command of Lt. General Simon Bolivar Buckner.

The landings were good, a soft but beautiful assault. No dead or wounded; not even a burning or wrecked vehicle on the beach. An appropriate invasion for a Holy Day, Easter Sunday. But as it is in life, all good things must come to an end. Our forces were soon to catch hell. The Jap was well aware that Okinawa was a new staging area, and the last stop for the Allies before they landed on their road to Japan.

Okinawa, estimated to be sixty times the size of Iwo, garrisoned about 100,000 troops, commanded by General Mitsuru Ushijima.

General Ushijima's Command, an assemblage of the Japanese 32nd Army being reinforced by the 44th Independent brigade, 24th Infantry Division was well equipped and trained, but not as yet bloodied. Then there was the 62nd Infantry Division, the 27th Tank Regiment, having as its heaviest armament a 57MM gun; and artillery units, mortar and Naval units, assorted repair service units, and a Native Okinawan Home Guard with an estimated 17,000–20,000 men. An additional 1,700 Okinawan male students, fourteen years of age and older, were organized into volunteer youth groups.

Formidable forces, each with a dedicated cause.

General Ushijima, with Tokyo's urging, proposed to take a heavy toll on the Allies, both in manpower and in delay, with hopes of gaining time that would be helpful in the expected assault of the homeland. Ushijima was equipped to fight a war of attrition. He had substantial weaponry and a large defensive army trained in and schooled in guerrilla warfare. Ushijima allowed our American forces a soft landing at the beaches. He preferred to make his stand at his prepared major defense line in the south, the Shuri Line, where he had a natural barrier of jagged ridges, some rising to a height of 300 feet. We soon started to pay a price, a hell of a price, for this starting area.

On the small island of Le Shima, three miles from Okinawa, our armed forces, the fighting GIs, lost a dear friend, the Pulitzer Prizewinning columnist, Ernie Pyle. A Jap sniper got him; Ernie took one in the head. General Buckner, Commander Tenth Army, was killed by a Jap 47 MM anti-tank shell when he went to an observation post to observe Tank–Infantry Operations.

16: Okinawa and Leyte—Giant Steps

Okinawa, when captured, would provide us with an excellent base to train and stage final operations for the assault on the Japanese homeland.

Kyushu, the southernmost island of Japan, was only 350 nautical miles away. Okinawa also had numerous airbase sites which meant trouble for Japan. The Japanese High Command not only intended to defend Okinawa, but also to destroy our war ships and supply vessels that would be needed in our invasion of their homeland. So the Japs fell back on thousands of young volunteers, instilled with the Bushido Code and ready to die for their Emperor and homeland. The Japs began forming a Corps of Kamikaze (The Divine Storm), poorly trained men, to be converted by their country into human bombs—suicide pilots. They would be flung, wave after wave, in a desperate measure of counter-attack against our forces. *Ten Go* (Heavenly Operation) meant the expending of Japan's finest young men flying any plane that could fly with a bomb attached. Hundreds of planes were assembled at the airfields of the home islands of Kyushu, Shikoku and Honshu. Trained pilots with the best of planes were assigned an escort. The veteran pilot would guide the Kamikaze to their targets and then return. About 1,815 planes with sufficient fuel for just a one-way flight were assigned to carry out the well-planned and carefully organized attacks on our fleet at Okinawa.

During the first few days of April, we sustained at an alarming rate damaged and sunken ships. Our Naval casualties mounted.

Our Ground Forces, after a soft beachhead, moved inland and encountered the Shuri Line; General Ushijima's defensive line.

The blood flowed freely; the body count, after an eighty-three day battle, was: 110,000 Japanese killed, 10,755 taken prisoner.

The United States Army and Marines suffered 7,613 killed and missing, 31,807 wounded and 26,211 other casualties.

United States Naval Personnel suffered 4,320 killed and 7,312 wounded.

Okinawa was declared secure on June 21, 1945. The Kamikazes had flown 1,809 sorties and lost 930 aircraft. The Japs sank seventeen of our ships and damaged 198, including twelve carriers and ten battleships.

The long arm of Fate pointed south and beckoned us to fulfill our assignment as Reserve Units for Okinawa.

It was April 13, 1945. To the south of Iwo and Okinawa, in our peaceful secluded war zone sector of the South Pacific, New Caledonia, the Army informed us of the death of President Franklin Delano Roosevelt, of a cerebral hemorrhage at the age of sixty-three, in Warm Springs, Georgia.

All training stopped. The Army gave us a day off to mourn and/or to get our thoughts together.

New orders: embark to Okinawa.

We worked in shifts for two days and nights water-proofing and loading our tanks. Our wounded who were fit for duty were returned to our outfit. Our new replacement tanks were unavailable. The worn-out barrel of our tank was not replaced; we had to go with what we had.

Our new Tank Commander, Kambell, was pale and very tense. "Soup", the moniker that was placed on this Lieutenant Kambell, presented me with a bottle of American whiskey, part of his monthly officer's ration, stating that this whiskey was for the crew, adding that it would be medicine in combat. We boarded our LST and shipped out as ready as we could be to go to war.

Our "cruise" to Okinawa gave us time to be briefed on the Pacific War to date. The Army notified us that it was touch-and-go in the Okinawan Campaign, that is why the reserves—us—were being ordered in.

The Army gave us a refresher course concerning our enemy, the Jap. We were reminded that the greatest honor the Jap could attain was to die for his Emperor, according to the Bushido Code. We dealt with the fanaticism of the Japanese forces in our battle in the Palaus, the Iwo Jimo Campaign, and the problems that the Allies had encountered with the Jap troops and the Japanese civilians on the island of Saipan in the Marianas. To the horror of the American GIs, they witnessed hundred of Japanese women and men committing suicide. The Japanese civilian population and military personnel were brainwashed into believing—and believed—that the Americans were savages who would rape, torture and desecrate woman and children. Our men saw parents bash out the brains of their babies, brothers kill their sisters. Fathers slit mothers' throats and they were powerless to stop this useless and stupid slaughter. Japanese soldiers threatened the civilians who desired to live and jumped off the cliffs with them to their deaths.

That was what we could expect from the Japanese people. Okinawa, the last island barrier to the Jap homeland, contained a large civilian population.

Our voyage to Okinawa gave us time to reflect, analyze and attempt to foresee what Fate had in store. Our conclusion: we could not change Fate, we had to go with the current and take things as they came, one at a time.

The Army provided for us; they directed us on how to do it, when to do it. But the Army never told us why we should do it—just do it.

The Army also paid us for being the takers of human lives... killers.

Fate took charge of our destinies.

I guess you could and would say our lives were sweet and simple.

But... the crew of the United States Army Tank C5, 710th Tank Battalion, had a problem. A conference was called; the agenda: what was to be done with "our treasure", the bottle of booze? I suggested that we concur with "Soup" Kambell, the donator of our treasure, and save the booze to be used as medicine and for medicinal purposes in combat, noting that if we worked it right, we, the crew, could be the recipients of additional bottles, maybe a bottle a month. It appeared to be a long and hard battle forthcoming, and we could use the booze.

Lightning took issue with my position, stating that we would probably get it on Okinawa. A bird in the hand is worth two in the bush—let's drink it and tell Soup his bottle of booze broke in transit if needs be. Bill and Ike supported my stand.

Lightning should have kicked me in the rump. We then could have drunk and enjoyed Soup's booze.

On May 7, 1945, while aboard ship we received the good news. Germany had surrendered, VE Day: now the European GIs could come to our Pacific Paradise and give us a hand—a big hand, which was needed to invade the Jap homeland.

Good news comes in bunches. Reprieve: our Tenth Army had penetrated and broken General Ushijima's defensive positions and were moving inland.

We were released from our Reserve Assignment and rerouted to the island of Leyte, in the Philippine Islands.

Landing May 17, 1945, we began the task of establishing a new camp on an isolated peninsular just off the mainland, about two miles from Tacloban, one of the landing beachheads for General MacArthur's invasion of Leyte. Our new campsite, though secluded, developed into what in broad terms could be called a tropical Paradise. The blue Pacific Ocean, with a long sandy white beach was our front yard, and a small body of water separated us from the mainland. A constant breeze soothed us and made sleep pleasant.

Our camp was laid out in four rows of pyramidal tents, with Headquarters Platoon facing the ocean on the beach. My platoon, the First, was behind Headquarters and facing the Company's assembly area. Directly across from us and facing us was the Second Platoon; behind them, the Third Platoon facing inland. Men of our Company who had the knowledge of carpentry with the assistance of Area Philippines built a Mess Hall. It was furnished with Philippine mahogany tables and benches, we could now consume our chow down while seated.

As could be expected, the officers demanded their own Officers' Mess. Their demands were met, a separate Officers' Mess was built, to serve as a mess hall and Officers' Club.

The officers, through a process of conscription, selected the best of Battalion cooks and they now had to cook for them, the officers.

The process of feeding the troops taken care of, the next order of business was establishing and building a latrine. This was no longer a slit dug into the ground to be straddled while attempting to relieve yourself of your bodily excrements. A building semi-enclosed by palm leafs with a roof and sit-down facilities was built. The Army, while providing for our needs, also reminded us that there was a war to be won.

Our motor pool, the area where our tanks and other vehicles were stored, was established. We were back to work maintaining our tanks.

The happy and smiling Lieutenant "Soup" comes back to the Company scene. He approaches our tank and says, "Hi, how are things going?" I respond in kind. Then Soup says, "Remember the bottle of whiskey that I wanted you to care of while in transit? I want it now."

I reminded our Lieutenant that the booze was medicine for his crew. Soup declared emphatically, "No way! It is my whiskey and I want it back—now."

I climbed the tank, entered the turret, and retrieved our treasured booze from its hiding place. Standing in the turret's opening, yelling loudly and clearly so everyone in the motor pool could hear, I shouted, "Lieutenant Kambell—here is your fuckin' booze! Shove it up your fuckin' ass!" I then told Kambell that if he wanted the booze to climb up on the tank and get it. He did. From then on, Lieutenant Kambell, our Tank Commander, was no longer called Soup. His new moniker was now "Wee Willie".

Back at our base, we were really living it up in the lap of luxury. Our Company appropriated an electrical generator and wire for conducting electrical energy. After wiring, our tents now had lighting. Barrels containing water were rigged up on a platform. The tropical sun heated the water, and we now had hot showers in the afternoons and early evening. The water pumped out of the ground was brackish, and most of us preferred the ocean for bathing and recreation. The Army issued each GI with a heavy cotton bag. In Army nomenclature this bag was called a mattress cover. It was highly valued by the Filipinos, and on the barter or exchange system redeemable for a twelve-ounce bottle of corn whiskey. The GIs' ingenuity found that by filling our mattress covers with air they now had an excellent air mattress for surfboarding, a new and exciting way to pass the time.

Our scrounger "got" a wooden Navy whaleboat. After devising a sail, we now had a yacht. Sailing with the ocean breeze was exhilarating, but tacking back against the wind was time-consuming. Oh, yes, our "Skipper" was Karle, a misplaced "sailor" from Wisconsin. Our dirty clothes were laundered by Filipino girls.

Because of these girls being available, the Army restarted its Hygienic Indoctrination. Our looey, Wee Willie, was designated instructor. The crux of his counseling was how to apply a condom on a broom handle.

The Army always furnished us with entertainment. We were amused by Bob Hope and his troupe in Louisiana and Hawaii. Here on Leyte we had our nightly movies, plus a disc jockey piping in music and honoring all requests. The Pacific edition of the *Yank* magazine arrived monthly. But, the best entertainment was Wee Willie and his hygiene class. That was my boy, Willie.

Living Army garrison-style in a rear staging area also had its problems; all was not a rose garden. We had to contend with our Wee Willies and also our "heroes" who were now pulling their heads out of their holes. A notable "hero", our whistle-blowing Sergeant, was again making his presence felt.

Precautionary health measures were being taken by The Army. Amoebic dysentery was discovered to be prevalent. This was an infectious inflammatory disease of the colon, resulting in severe pain and diarrhea. I was one of its victims and required to be injected with a very strong and potent serum. Orders were to rest (light duty) on the day we were treated.

As was to be expected, the Sarge blew his police whistle and the Company fell out into the assembly area. The men lined up with the Sarge's back to me as I reclined on my cot obeying the Army's order to rest. Apparently some of the guys laughed or whatever. The Sarge turned, scowled and barked, "Luzinas, get your ass out here, you're no better than anyone else!"

I resented that inference, so I barked back at him, "Go to hell, you know that I am on light duty!" Now it's a known fact in the Army that you don't score brownie points that way. The Army's advice and directive is to obey the order, then complain. Who cared? After meditating in the woods in Caledonia, my final analysis was that Fate decreed my destiny: death, be it by the Jap or whatever. So I planned on enjoying my remaining time allotted to me on this earth. I would work with and for my tank crew. As far as the Army and its crap was concerned, I would do no more and probably much less.

Taking into consideration the other experiences of our "Army

Careers", our presence on this Pacific Paradise, Leyte, was truly enjoyable and memorable; but, the reason for us being there, war— *the war*—still existed, and was on full burner.

The Jap homelands were bombed, demolished daily by hundreds of B29s. The Jap had gathered 10,000 airplanes that were to be used in Kamikaze attacks when we landed as the invaders. Three million troops and twenty-eight million civilians were being trained in the usage of weapons... Teenage girls were provided with improvised weapons of pointed bamboo poles and pitchforks and told that if they did not kill at least one of the enemy, they didn't deserve to live. Our B29s continued their daylight bombing raids, blasting sixteen square miles of Tokyo and devastating the cities of Yokohama and Nagoya.

On July 15, 1945, President Truman met with Winston Churchill and Josef Stalin in a devastated Berlin in the suburb of Potsdam, for a Summit meeting, dealing with a conquered Germany and a war-shattered Europe. At this Potsdam Conference, President Truman also intended to issue an Allied ultimatum to the Japanese, demanding unconditional surrender.

On July 16, the agreement of China's Generalissimo Chiang Kai-Shek's reached Potsdam. That night, the Potsdam Proclamation, which threatened "utter devastation of the Japanese homeland" unless Japan surrendered unconditionally, was broadcast worldwide. Tokyo monitors picked up the proclamation. Prime Minister Suzuki and his associates studied the Allied demands. Suzuki told reporters, "The Potsdam Proclamation, in my opinion, is just a rehash of the Cairo Declaration, and the Government does not consider it of great importance."

Several Japanese newspapers, in defiance of the Government-imposed censorship of the Proclamation, declared it "a laughable matter... since the joint declaration of America, Britain and Chungking is of no great moment, it will merely serve to re-enhance the Government's resolve to carry the war forward to a successful conclusion."

The war went on, and it would now be necessary to invade Japan. Unbeknownst to us, the first landings, planned for November 1, 1945, would involve 767,600 men on the island of Kyushu, the southernmost and third largest (13,770 square miles) of the four main islands of Japan. This was named "Operation Olympic", and we were scheduled to be with the first wave of the invading Allied Forces.

The attack and invasion on Honshu and Tokyo was planned for March 1946. Noting the resistance the Allies had encountered on other Pacific Islands, the planners of these operations anticipated heavy casualties, over one million for The Olympic Operation alone.

Activities were stepped up. Our refresher exercises of Tank-Infantry Tactics took us to the Ormoc Mountains on the northwestern areas of Leyte. This area, with the Ormoc Valley and Breakneck Ridge, was the battleground and the scene of the toughest fighting in the Leyte Campaign. On August 6, 1945, our Infantry unit was being shown how to direct our tank's firepower from and with a telephone located in the rear of the tank.

Prior to our undertaking of these exercises the "Old Man"—our Company Commander—ordered us not to destroy palm trees, as these were owned by soap companies back in the States, and our Government had to reimburse the soap companies for any damaged or destroyed trees.

Our first "schooling" was successfully completed. Hoping to obtain a breather for the rest of the day, we hurried and cleaned our guns. Our guns cleaned, we resumed the GI's favorite pastime; goofing off and shooting the bull. Our pleasure was soon to be cut short. Approaching was our "peacock", Wee Willie. He stopped in front of us and stated, "Luzinas, I want you to fire your guns for another demonstration."

I curtly told Willie, "My guns were fired today, they were cleaned and are clean." I went on, "Lieutenant, you have other guns in your platoon, they haven't fired their guns, use one of them."

Lieutenant Kambell then gave me a direct order. "You are to fire your guns!"

I replied, "Oh! Is that the kind of game we are playing?"

Lightning and I mounted up and entered the turret. We remounted the 30 caliber MG and took care of other necessary details prior to the firing of our guns. Our 75 was bore-sighted on our first problem, so it did not require realignment. Bill and Ike climbed in. Wee Willie got in the turret and directed Bill to the site where we were to exhibit our gunnery skills. Willie dismounted from the tank and instructed the Infantry on the usage of the tank's weaponry.

Climbing back into the tank, Willie started surveying our front with his binoculars. After a time, he asked me if I could locate the simulated gun emplacement. After scanning our front with the tank's telescope, I reported to Willie that I was unable to locate the so-called enemy emplacement. Willie then ordered me to traverse my guns and inquired whether I could see the highest palm tree to our front.

I told Willie that I had good vision of the tree, but, I still could not locate the simulated gun position.

Willie then gave me a fire order. "Knock down the tree with cannon fire."

I turned, facing Willie, and then informed him, "Lieutenant, our orders are to not damage or destroy palm trees."

Willie sneered at me, "I am giving you a direct order. Knock down that palm tree!"

Obeying that order, I located the tree with my 30 caliber MG fire, made my corrections and fired an HE round at my target. The round found the target, severed the tree trunk, and the palm tree was knocked down. Our firing of my guns for the Infantry was ended.

Willie, prior to exiting the tank, asked me what I was going to tell the Captain (CO) about destroying the palm tree. I looked him in the eye and told him, "Lieutenant, that is your problem. What are *you* going to tell the Old Man?"

Willie dismounted the tank. After securing our guns, I climbed out of the turret to the engine deck and proceeded to get some water from my canteen, which was hanging from the radio antenna, outside and to the rear of the turret. My canteen with its water was missing; in its place was an empty canteen, World War I issue. I examined and opened the canteen. It stunk like a cesspool from booze. Scratched on the bottom of the canteen was "O" and a series of numbers of which I took to be an officer's Army serial number. Knowing that our crew would never attempt to pull off this shit, I recognized the work of Wee Willie. Our Army had brainwashed us into believing that a Commissioned Officer is a gentlemen and should be treated with respect. Our Lieutenant Kambell was a crook, a cheap-booze-guzzling, petty larceny jerk.

The theft of a GI's water ration in Pacific Combat was strictly forbidden, a cardinal sin.

Still atop the engine deck, I faced Willie who was on the ground and yelled at him, "Which one of you sons of bitches stole my water?" No response.

I then pointed my finger at Willie, and again inquired, "Which one of you sons of bitches stole my water?"

Willie finally responded; he ordered me to dismount. As I faced him with my legs astride, Willie informed me that I was talking to an officer—stand at attention. I told him to go to hell. "When I see the Company Commander, he will tell me who and what is an officer."

There was a loud cheer from the Infantry. A jubilant GI then told us that the Allies had dropped a bomb, one bomb equivalent to the bombing raids of two thousand B29s, on Japan. All activity ceased; I left Willie standing there and returned to my crew to discuss this happy turn of events.

Returning to our bivouac encampment, I gave Lightning Wee Willie's canteen and told him to protect it with his life if necessary; he did.

I then shaved and waited for the call. It took longer than I expected, but it came. The Company Clerk popped his head into our tent and said, "Ed, the Old Man wants you."

I went in saluting. "Corporal Luzinas reporting as ordered, Sir."

The Captain returned my salute and started his reprimand, "Luzinas, you are the best gunner in the Company..." And he talked and chewed me out as a father talks to a misbehaving son. I stood at a relaxed attention, he never called me on it to stand at attention. After a short monologue, he stated that Lieutenant Kambell wanted me court-martialed. Then he asked, "What in the hell is going on?"

I informed the Company Commander of the day's events and told the Captain that I would take a court martial. I then said, "I cannot and I shall not go to war with that guy. I want out of that guy's tank."

The Old Man pounded his field desk with his hand and told me that I was no longer in Lieutenant Kambell's tank; he stated that as of now I was the gunner in his tank, I was his gunner. He told me to get back in line and then dismissed me.

The crew was waiting for my return in the tent. I told them, no court martial, but I was no longer their gunner. I told the crew that the Old Man was patronizing me. But... there would be repercussions.

I asked if they'd received any word of this bomb that was dropped. "Nothing as yet," was their reply. "But if it's true it could be the end of our war."

Knowing the Jap, and after our experiences with him in the Palaus, we hoped and prayed that the Jap would quit. It has to be noted that within our crew and others in our platoon there weren't any verbal cries of jubilation, just silent hope.

It was August 7, 1945, eastern side of International Date Line (August 6, stateside).

President Truman's statement to the United States by commercial radio and to Japan by short wave told the world that the bomb ("Little Boy") was an Atomic Bomb. The Potsdam Ultimatum of July 26 was issued to spare the Japanese people utter destruction. If they (the Japs) did not accept our terms, they may expect a rain of ruin from the air the like of which has never been seen on this earth.

There wasn't any response from the Japanese. The military in the Japanese Cabinet refused to budge. Newspapers and radios were only permitted to speak vaguely of a "new type" of bomb and extensive damage in Hiroshima, the city bombed. A *Domei* News Agency Reporter who witnessed the detonation of the bomb reported that at 8:16 A.M., one or two enemy planes flew over Hiroshima and dropped one or two bombs completely destroying the city with casualties estimated at 170,000 dead.

We at Leyte were still expecting the Japs to cease and surrender. All training stopped. Our Company Commander sent two GIs down the road about a mile from encampment with a walkie-talkie and orders to notify the Company if the Battalion Commander approached. If notified, all men were told to be engaged in some activity. Was peace around the corner?

Even with these epoch-making world events, our Commissioned Officers' egos still had to be appeased. No court martial, no demotion in rank, but guard duty. I was ordered to walk sentry duty in the boondocks. No sweat, I walked two hours, then had four hours off, for a twenty-four hour period.

On August 8 the Japanese Foreign Minister, Tojo, in desperation sent a message to Ambassador Naotake Sato in Moscow, to have Moscow mediate an end to the war.

In an appointment with Russia's Foreign Minister, Vyacheslav Molotov, Sato was formally handed a notification in the name of the Soviet Union. The heart of this statement: "On August ninth, the Soviet Union will consider itself in a state of war with Japan."

In the United States, President Truman, recognizing his "terrible responsibility" for the suffering at Hiroshima, stated the Japanese had not surrendered, or even hinted at surrender. A second bomb was scheduled for delivery on August 9, and a third and fourth bomb if necessary. The second bomb, "Fat Boy", fell at 11:01 A.M. on the Japanese Island of Kyushu, in the city of Nagasaki, on August 9. How many of the Japanese died has never been determined. Estimates of deaths as a result of the Fat Boy were 140,000. The bombs of Hiroshima and Nagasaki demolished centers of war industry and turned them to blackened wastelands. Officials in Nagasaki wrote their city was like a graveyard, with not a tombstone left standing.

An emergency meeting of the Japanese Supreme Council of War was convened mid-morning of August 9. Council Members, having had to contend with the Hiroshima catastrophe, were now faced with a new dilemma: the emergence of Soviet troops into Japanese-held Manchuria. Prime Minister Suzuki hoped to have and use this meeting with the intention of Japan accepting the Surrender Ultimatum of the Potsdam Summit. The War Council was presented with word of the Nagasaki bombing.

The Militants in the Council held onto the hope of "Heavenly Intervention". Japan would repel us Americans, just as the Mongol ships in the year 1281 were repelled by "the Divine Wind".

The Peace Faction of the Council were convinced that nothing in heaven or earth could save Japan.

Two hours of arguments were heard and held by opposing factions before the meeting of the Japanese Supreme Council of War broke off.

A unanimous vote of the War Council was required before the War Council could agree to the Potsdam surrender terms.

The fate of 100 million Japanese had to be decided quickly before we dropped the third bomb on a nation that had never known defeat. For six torturous days the two factions bickered. A heroic figure was needed to quell the discord. A totally unexpected figure—truly a savior of the Japanese nation—took command.

17: Peace

In Japan's hour of crisis, Emperor Hirohito intervened. Addressing the War Council, the Emperor, after a short summation, declared the time has come to bear the unbearable. "I swallow my tears and give sanction to the proposal to accept the Allied Proclamation," stated the Emperor. On August 10 each Cabinet Member of the six-man Supreme Council for the Direction of War signed a statement accepting the Potsdam Proclamation on the condition that "the Supreme Power of the Emperor" not be compromised. The fanatical element of the Japanese Army persisted in their continuance of the war. A bogus message was broadcast to the troops to fight on resolutely.

On Leyte, the Army still inflicted its wrath upon me; I was assigned guard duty again.

But the United States Army showed its fairness, and displayed a bit of democracy. I was informed that Lieutenant Kambell, our Wee Willie Platoon Leader of the First Platoon, was no longer with us. The Army had shipped him out for reassignment. The reception of this news and the signs of the end of our war with Japan began a week of celebrating. The First Platoon was shed of its misfit Willie, and shortly we would be returning to the States and home.

The news of Willie and whatever I believed of its interpretation was good. Still, the Army wanted its pound of flesh. I walked my rounds of guard duty in the Ormoc Hills. My thoughts: the Jap made his last stand on Leyte in this region; if a diehard Jap straggler was concealed in the heavy foliage that surrounded my post, he—the Jap—could take me out in a hurry, and I would be one of the last casualties of the Pacific War. I did not want that recognition or distinction.

On August 10 (Washington time) President Truman received the message of Foreign Minister Tojo. The message was clear:

The Japanese Government is ready to accept the terms enumerated in the joint declaration issued at Potsdam on July 26, 1945, with an understanding that said declaration does not compromise any demand which prejudices the prerogatives of His Majesty as Sovereign Ruler.

President Truman had been demanding surrender without conditions, and yet the Jap stubbornly imposed one. President Truman, after convening and conferring with his Cabinet, directed Secretary of State Byrnes to draft a response to the Japanese message.

Secretary of State Byrnes' proposed answer went as follows:

From the moment of surrender, the Authority of the Emperor and the Japanese Government to rule the State shall be subject to the Supreme Commander of Allied Powers, who will take such steps as he deems necessary to effectuate the surrender terms. The ultimate form of government of Japan will be established by the freely expressed will of the Japanese people.

With that message Byrnes had reassured the Japanese concerning the Sovereignty of the Emperor.

President Truman approved and ordered it to be submitted to the Allies for approval.

All but Russia accepted. The Soviets insisted they share the Allied High Command in occupied Japan and demanded veto power in the selection of a Supreme Commander. After the rejection of the Soviet demands, the Russians backed down and agreed to Byrnes' message.

Upon receiving the Allies' message, Emperor Hirohito stressed the clause calling for Japan's ultimate form of government to be set by the freely expressed will of the people, and pointed out that it could be the end of the Monarchy. He stated it would be useless if the people did not want an Emperor. He thought it all right to leave it to the people.

The Japanese Cabinet, after discussion of the message, were still at an impasse. The peace element wanted to accept the terms and the Military element sought to reject them and fight to the bitter end. The bickering and impasse continued. By August 14, Emperor Hirohito realized that time was running out. He would on his own authority summon an Imperial Conference of the Cabinet. If there were still signs of dissention, he, the Emperor, would command surrender.

Addressing the conference, Hirohito stated, "I want you all to agree to my conclusions. We cannot continue with war any longer. It is my desire that all of you, my Ministers of State, bow to my wishes and accept the Allied reply. It is my desire that the Cabinet at once draw up a Imperial Rescript to end the war."

In a short period of time, the Japanese Foreign Ministers sent a note to the Allied nations through embassies in Switzerland that Japan had accepted their conditions of surrender.

After the shedding of blood, sweat and tears, the global conflict was finally over.

Peace was about to return to the world.

18: Reflections

It was official: President Truman's announcement at 7:00 P.M. Eastern Wartime on Tuesday August 14, 1945... Japan had surrendered. The war in the Pacific was over. We had out-played Fate for the present, and hopefully the United States and home were our destinations. The celebrating began; the Company rats, knowing that the Army and its system would again protect them, pulled their heads out of their holes and were no longer afraid for their vulnerable fannies. The shooting was over and they could resume pushing their stripes around—and they did.

The men of our outfit gathered up their buddies and gave silent but thoughtful thanks that it was over.

Lightning, Ike and I brought two bottles of corn and went into the outskirts of our Ormoc Mountain Encampment and drank, enjoyed the new turn of events: Peace. We kicked (discussed) the highlights of our almost three-year military "careers" and tried to foresee what the future held in store. We were in complete agreement that once home and settled we would get together for a real celebration, thick steaks and the works.

This dream was not to be: Fate intervened.

The victory celebration by our troops had to end. We had to come back down to earth and resume life, now as peace-time soldiers located in the Ormoc Mountains on the island of Leyte, Philippine Islands. We were thousands of miles from the United States and home. The realization hit us; there were millions of GIs in the same predicament and we all had to sweat it out until transport arrived—a ship to return us home.

The Army did the next best thing. They ordered us to our home away from home—the beach near Dulag and Tacloban. Abandoning our tank, we drove our tanks to our motor pool area on the beach, covered them with their tarpaulins and left them for the Army Ordinance. Our Tank, C5, 710th Tank Battalion, named Champagne, served us well, but we were glad to be rid of her.

We were now peacetime GIs on a lonely remote island in the Pacific Ocean with a lot of time on our hands, praying for a ship and stateside.

Our Government set up a system, a fair system, to bring her gallant and successful warriors home. They devised a point system based on length of service, service done overseas, and additional points for meritorious awards. GIs awarded the highest points had first preference. So, we awaited our turn and our ship.

We now had to endure our new predicament, that of GIs in a non-combatant mode, away from home with limited Army routine, with unrestricted free time uninhibited by officers, both the commissioned and non-commissioned. We could live with that and enjoy it, but still we wanted our ship. Our peacetime Army duty: guard and KP (kitchen police). They would catch me for both. We were no sooner settled in on the beach when our whistle-happy First Sergeant stuck me with guard duty. Guard wasn't bad, even enjoyable in a sense; it occupied part of my day and two memorable events occurred.

The first was while patrolling the Commissioned Officers' Area in the dead of night. I heard a scream from one of the officer's tents. Remembering the rumor that someone was cutting up GIs with a machete, I went to investigate.

The officers were up, excited and in a turmoil; one of their kind had problems. The problem—it wasn't someone chopping up an officer, a centipede had bitten this Officer and Gentlemen's penis!

During my daylight tour of the Battalion's perimeter, I encountered a screeching monkey, a GI's pet tethered to a run with a dog trying to catch him. I chased the dog away and found a new friend. The monkey jumped into my arms and perched on my shoulder. The monkey's owner came to see what the commotion was all about. As the owner reached for his monkey, my buddy the monkey started screeching at him—protecting me; and people say animals are dumb.

Oh yes, clearing up the cutting of military personnel; a GI cook on one of the islands went berserk and cut up some GIs in the dead of the night on one of the islands with his kitchen butcher's knife. He was caught and received medical treatment.

The war over, the 710th Tank Battalion was no longer needed, nor apparently wanted. We gathered in an open area on the beach and, entertaining the proper Army formality, the 710th Tank Battalion was officially deactivated. We, as an organized unit, no longer existed in the United States Army records.

The Quartermaster unit in Leyte must have believed that the 710 was dissipated, as our incoming food rations new consisted of C-Rations and macaroni.

The Army flooded the Battalion with Government Printing Office educational manuals and a few comic books. After deactivation, our Company's commissioned officers disappeared taking the comic books with them. Our officers, I guess, believed in the old adage "out of sight, out of mind", and that was the course to follow. They, the officers, probably had their reasons. Well, the officers passed down to the enlisted men dog-eared and very well read comic books after a while. Our rations for our sustenance being below par, our cooks had to make use of all their talents to make our food palatable.

The rotation system, based on points, finally starting taking hold. Our mess Sergeant and his First Cook were relocated to another unit being assembled to ship back to the States. Our cooks were lucky; we were not. The Cook's Helper was promoted to Mess Sergeant (Staff), and he took charge. His skill was lacking and his chow was less than desirable. Our Battalion Commander started making the scene after chow and checking the slop buckets (garbage cans); they were full to the overflowing. We existed and survived on C-rations.

Our First Sergeant and Ollie got the rotation call, having the required points. Our Platoon, the First, had its Sergeant promoted to the Company's First Sergeant. Buck Sergeant Karle was moved up to Staff and acquired the responsibilities of the First Platoon Sergeant.

I was back in the Army again. The Army carried on with its crap, but now we had a new author.

My old Platoon Sergeant, now First Sergeant, carried on with the Army's policy of slapping my wrist. Guard Duty again. My new post—guarding Red Cross personnel. While doing my duty at this Red Cross Entertainment Center, the opportunity arose to procure (or in the GI jargon, "appropriate") Cola syrup from which soda pop is made. Obtaining about three gallons in a water can, I found our nectar too heavy to carry. But the Sergeant of the Guard, with the use of the Guard Jeep, delivered my booty right to the front entrance of my tent. This guard duty of the Red Cross facility proved to be a fruitful assignment. Our beer allotment was cut to two cans a month, and my cola syrup compensated for the shortage of beer. We now had flat, warm, flavored water to drink. We worked on that; no luck, it was still warm.

Mother nature now proceeded in giving us a taste of her power of vengeance—a typhoon. All our tents were secured, and we were forced to wear our metal helmets while out in the open to protect us from the coconuts that were falling from the violently swaying palm trees. No casualties, some damage to our tents; but our beautiful beach was now piled four feet high with seaweed washed ashore by the high surf of the ocean created by the winds of the typhoon!

They didn't catch me for guard, but clean-up now.

Sergeant Alvin pulled his head out of his hole, now he was assigned to be in charge of the clean-up detail. As to be expected, we had a disagreement or dispute. Alvin informed or squealed to the First Sergeant, KP (kitchen police), this time. While fulfilling my "punishment" I offered some suggestions to the man preparing the chow on how to make the food edible. The suggestions improved the food. The "cook" told the First Sergeant, who in turn asked me to cook for the Company. My reply was, "Sarge, are you kidding? I'm on KP, remember? There is no way that I'm going to cook! If you can eat this crap, so can I."

The original Cadre of our Unit now had sufficient points for rotation, and they moved out. This last rotation was very beneficial to the guys still left in C Co.

Karle, a recruit like the rest of us back in Polk, now a Staff Sergeant, was promoted to First Sergeant. First Sergeant Karle obtained two men from the ranks who had culinary skills. There was now a vast improvement in our chow. These two prepared edible chow with the sustenance provided by our Quartermaster. The Army's policy of nit-picking and petty punishment ceased. Guard and kitchen duties were strictly adhered to by the duty roster.

As the absence of our commissioned officers was noticeable, the responsibility of Company Command was placed on Karle's shoulders.

The long wait for our ship, the stress, the inactivity, and the dreams of home and loved ones started taking their toll. The guys were edgy and irritable; there were many squabbles and a few fist fights. Men started cracking up. One flipped, had to be restrained and hospitalized. Another sat on the beach and continually stared to the east. His buddy tended to him, bringing chow and water.

I was not bored from inactivity; the Army would not allow me that privilege. But our ship and rotation would be a blessing.

We had turned in our weapons and other equipment that was of no use. The required processing for re-entry in the United States was underway. GIs from other units gathered with us to sail on the same ship.

The GI quartered in our tent must have been a Texan, he came in with his guitar—yes, a guitar. His days were spent serenading me with his yodeling. It was a bit much, I did not need that so I started spending my days on the beach.

On December 24, 1945, the day before Christmas, our Christmas present from Uncle Sam arrived—our ship was in port.

Leaving the tents and Army cots, we departed our Garden of Eden and boarded ship. It was another wartime cruise ship built for and used to transport bananas, not people. Our cruise of twenty-three days, an ocean voyage of about eight thousand miles to the United States, began. Leaving the gangway and stepping aboard, I felt that Fate was playing another cruel trick. The men, the Army, stated the war was over. I did not believe I was alive, and could the war really have ended? After being assigned to a fart sack, as Naval men called their specially designed sleeping bunks, I noted that our location was in a hold packed with humanity. Before we even got underway the heat and stagnant air was overwhelming. After getting squared away, I went topside, joining Lightning, Ike and the others. We watched the island of Leyte disappear beyond the horizon and prepared for shipboard existence again. With darkness came confirmation: the war was really over. On the ocean's horizon a ship, a lightened ship, the first I'd seen during all of our travels, came under way in the opposite direction.

With this sighting, all of my disbeliefs evaporated. The War was really over.

With morning came breakfast; oatmeal, hard cooked eggs with their shells on, and coffee. There was an abundance of eggs and we were advised to take extra to sustain us for lunch—we did. We were back to shipboard routine, breakfast—dinner, no lunch. Our gang spent the daylight hours watching the ocean, shooting the bull, reading paperback novels or playing cards; and of course there was the perpetual and ongoing poker game.

Both Lightning and I, being short of funds and knowing that we would be in need of operating capital stateside, pooled our resources and I indulged in this game of chance-poker.

Playing very close and only betting on sure hands we accumulated forty dollars the first day, twenty dollars each. That was not enough. Remembering my run of gambling, that of winning one day and losing the next, we decided to keep the twenty: a bird in the hand is worth two in the bush, stop gambling.

Our evening chow consisted of meat, potatoes, and carrots in a watery gravy. It was tasteless, but substantial. We had freshly baked bread, which was delicious.

Come darkness we reserved our sleeping place topside by leaving our blankets there. Sleep was pleasant, with the fresh, cool air and a gentle movement of the ship.

Of course there was discomfort. There were crude conditions topside too, and a steel deck to lay on; you could not dig a cavity for your butt.

Our dreams were shattered by a rain squall and we ran to our holds and assigned sacks. The stench of the stagnant air—that of sweaty bodies and the odor of the breakfast egg—was too much. Luckily we were not served traditional Navy fart beans! Back topside, I found shelter from the squall, which was brief and ended shortly, and spent the remainder of the night there.

This was typical of the events and routine for the twenty-three days of our cruise.

This experience was not, I repeat was not, the Army and the GIs that I was familiar with: nobody complained!

19: Demobilization

January 16, 1946: on the skyline there she was, the United States of America; the Californian coastline with its rolling hills and mountains; the splendor of its warm sunshine reflecting upon the lush green foliage. Aboard ship, a beehive of activity, saying your goodbyes to the guys that you went to war with, embracing your buddies who were now more like your brothers. Locating Lightning and Ike, we bade each other fond adieus with the promise to get together.

Back in '43, our Government showed the world how it could mobilize its Armed Forces. Now our involvement in the Government's reverse procedure began—demobilization. The GIs wanted to get home. After foreign service of nineteen months and three days, it was time to see my loved ones.

The process of demobilization began, the GIs were separated into different units, each unit assigned and transferred to their proper and respective demobilization center located in their sectors of the United States. Our ship docked in San Pedro Harbor on the outskirts of Los Angeles.

Disembarking, we were greeted by a band playing its traditional music. The Red Cross supplied us with coffee and donuts. Carrying our duffel bags, we went under the portals that separated the dock from the wharf. This portal stated, "Under these portals pass the best damn soldiers in the world." I will buy that; they were right. As transient troops we were provided temporary quarters and allowed to unwind.

The time came for a victorious Army to wine and dine its troops. Appropriately, we, the victors, were served by the vanquished German prisoners of war. They did not wine us, but gave us tomato juice instead; but our steaks and dinner was delicious, with ice cream for dessert. The fresh milk and ice cream were too rich for my system. I got the GI runs.

The Army allocated the following day as our day. No scheduled activities, so I spent the day getting accustomed to dry land and civilized people, the civilians. The third day we were bussed to Burbank Airfield, placed on a plane and started on a nineteen-hour and three-thousand-mile flight to my Demobilization Center, Fort Dix in New Jersey. This nineteen-hour flight actually took three days, ending in Pittsburgh PA, when the Army placed me on a train which took me to Dix. Our first delay: forced down by weather in Amarillo, Texas, located in the panhandle in northern Texas. The temperature was hovering around zero. Being only a short time out of the equatorial heat and not acclimatized, I froze my ass. A short tour at Dix, and I was a civilian again.

Epilogue

Liberation Day: January 24, 1946. At the convenience of our Government I was discharged, Honorably, from the Army of the United States.

After presentation of the Replica, the Ruptured Duck, signifying that I have served our country, and receiving partial payment of my mustering-out pay, I was notified that for the next twenty-four hours, I was still under Army jurisdiction: behave!

After nearly three years of learning how to maim and kill the enemies of our country, we were released. Now the problem arose—could we cope with society and flow within the mainstream of civilian life? Our Government recognized that this could be a problem, and they passed a law, the GIs 52–20 Club.

This law allowed honorably discharged veterans to apply for and receive or collect twenty dollars a week for fifty-two weeks, or one year, with the intent and hope that the Veterans could have this time to unwind and become useful law-abiding citizens.

The intent and thought of this law was excellent, *but*... would this pittance compensate a GI for what could be a lifetime of recurring nightmares and the shedding of his Blood, Sweat, and Tears?

Reunions

In 1989, the 710th Tank Battalion celebrated and enjoyed its thirty-ninth Reunion.

Reunion events occurred in various cities in our Eastern States and Canada.

Memorable highlights of reunions I attended, some were notable and some laughable:

Major (BATT CO), now General, retired, USA, and Captain Harol, now Colonel, retired, USA, have attended the Battalion's Reunions. No other C Co. Commissioned Officers have made the scene.

Our whistle-happy First Sergeant is a Reunion Committee Member and attends all of our reunions. He, the First, has shown me an unmarked, unblemished 25 caliber (Jap Infantry rifle) bullet. The Sarge inquired if I remembered it? I told him no, and dropped this discussion. Note: the Sarge stated that this bullet was the one he took "when he got wounded". In reality he was never hit by or wounded by enemy fire. He would not even come up to the front where the shooting war was going on.

My naive lying and ignorance paid off. During our evening banquet the Sarge placed a bottle of Scotch on our table, good Scotch, aged top-shelf Scotch, and we enjoyed it.

The other non-coms, who had their heads in their holes, do not attend the reunions.

But... Fate and destiny were still playing their hands. Sgt. Sadler of Polk got killed in the war in Europe. Sgt. Hartley of Polk passed on at an early age. Ollie could never make contact. Bill, our driver, had problems with his health. Lightning (Forest Kern), had health problems. Harol, Ike and I enjoyed a C Co. reunion at Monroeville, PA. The 710th Tank Battalion had its own victory celebration. Karle and Don, members of the crew of our back-up tank, put on a Reunion to be remembered—the best. Prime porterhouse steaks, cut at least one and one-half inches thick, charbroiled to perfection by a Chef who basted the steaks with a Bourbon-garlic sauce. They did not serve tomato juice; we enjoyed fancy exhilarating beverages instead. Our Friday evening buffet table was laden with a gourmet selection of meats and cheeses with the appropriate trimmings.

We were provided with our own private and open bar, stocked with domestic and imported beverages, with wines for the ladies, and they provided beer. We, the old-timers, ate and drank from Friday night to Sunday morning.

Our free time on Saturday afternoon was spent touring the Wooster Ohio country and visiting an Amish settlement. This tour was on a bus that Don provided.

The Army's tank, Champagne, and its Combat Crew never did get together.

Out of our Tank Crew five surviving Peleliu, our roster shows:

One alcoholic victim

One emphysema casualty

One multiple sclerosis casualty.

Three crew members of five; WAS THAT FATE, OR WERE WE HEXED BY THE JAP?